WHAT PEOPLE SAY

"I have been receiving Bobby Simpson's "Thought for Tuesday" since 2007 and have always found a nugget or two regarding life lessons and our great game of Softball. I had the privilege of coaching against Bobby during my time with USA Softball and always treasured our time together. Bobby is a master teacher, motivator, and one heck of a human being that understands the importance of family, faith, and the process that leads to successful performance in the game and in life. I cannot wait to get my hands on *Thoughts For Tuesday: Gold Medal Wisdom For Life*."

Mike Candrea - Head Softball Coach, University of Arizona; Ten National Championships and over 1800 victories in more than forty years of coaching college softball; USA Olympic Coach, 2004 (Gold) and 2008 (Silver)

"Sports have always been more than just what we play on the field, but the personal life skills it teaches us. From the moment I met Bobby Simpson, he has a way of truly understanding the person versus just the talent he sees. His "Thoughts for Tuesday" help expand anyone around the game's knowledge of all that encompasses a great athlete, coach, clinician, or person and I am excited he will have the opportunity to continue to reach even more."

Jessica Mendoza - First female analyst for nationally televised Major League Baseball regular season and postseason games, plus radio broadcast of World Series games; analyst for NCAA Division I Women's College World Series; Former President at Women's Sports Foundation; Two-time Olympic Medalist

"Please keep the great thought-provoking emails coming from Higher Ground. I honestly look forward to opening my inbox to find your words of wisdom each Tuesday and I often use them in my team meetings at work."

Lawton Bassett - President of Ameris Bank

"I have enjoyed reading "Thought for Tuesday" items every week for over 10 years. What I find most remarkable about each item is the relatability and transferability, regardless of your season of life. These items are guiding principles and truths, grounded in faith, that have the potential to alter your perspective, thinking, and approach in the most positive way. These thoughts provide a weekly dose of authenticity that is tough to come by in today's world, but is so needed. No matter your age, gender, profession, or life circumstance, these thoughts will inspire you to be the very best version of you."

Kelley Bedrosian – Senior Project Lead, Learning and Development; Chick-fil-A, Inc.; Mercer University MBA; NCAA Athlete & Coach

"I've had the pleasure of learning from Bobby as a player under his leadership during my time on the British National Team and working with him through many Higher Ground Camps. Bobby has always found unique ways to deliver a message both efficiently and memorably. Even though I no longer play or coach, I continue to read his "Thoughts for Tuesdays" each week. The messages he sends are not only applicable to professional life, but they add to my spiritual growth as well. Sometimes his messages come just in time and lift me up or remind me of valuable life lessons I can apply immediately. I look forward to "Thoughts for Tuesday" each week, and I am excited to read a book full of Bobby and his thoughts!"

Megan M. Buning, PhD – Teaching Specialist II and Certified Mental Performance Consultant, Florida State University; Athletic Hall of Fame at University of South Carolina; SEC Women's Legends Member; Former NCAA Division I Coach

"You have always challenged me to see with extraordinary vision and look for the less than obvious. I pray God will allow me to constantly get better every day at the things that matter the most."

Jim Duggan - Pastor, Bellevue Baptist Church, Macon, GA

"From the first time I met Bobby at a coaches' clinic, I was impressed with his knowledge, his ability to teach, and his passion. I have read his "Thought for Tuesday" for years and they have provided me with many insights for my work. He has a spiritual orientation, but he also emphasizes that the athlete has to take responsibility to develop their "God-given" talents. He discusses so many issues that have applications on and off the field. I recommend this book to those who want to expand their perspective as coaches and as people."

Ken Ravizza, PhD - Sports Psychology Consultant; Professional teams including Chicago Cubs, LA Dodgers, LA Angels, Tampa Rays and NY Jets; Olympic teams including baseball, softball, water polo, figure skating; Consultant to U.S. Military Academy at West Point

"I always enjoy your weekly thoughts and pass them on to my players as well. I'm sure there are many more people whose lives you will influence in a positive manner."

Sheila Cornell Douty - Two-time Olympic Gold Medalist; member of USA National Softball Hall of Fame and International Softball Federation Hall of Fame

THOUGHTS FOR TUESDAY

GOLD MEDAL WISDOM FOR LIFE

BOBBY SIMPSON

Copyright © 2023 by Bobby Simpson. All rights reserved.

All rights reserved. No portion of this book may be reproduced in any form, stored in any retrieval system, or transmitted in any form or by any means—electronic, mechanical, photocopy, recording, scanning, or other—except for brief quotations in critical reviews or articles, without prior written permission of the publisher, except as provided by United States of America copyright law.

Published by Getting Better Everyday, Inc.
P.O. Box 741 Tifton, GA 31793

Scripture quotations marked (NKJV) are taken from the New King James Version®. Copyright © 1982 by Thomas Nelson. Used by permission. All rights reserved.

Scripture quotations marked (NIV) are taken from the THE HOLY BIBLE, NEW INTERNATIONAL VERSION®, NIV® Copyright © 1973, 1978, 1984, 2011 by Biblica, Inc.® Used by permission. All rights reserved worldwide.

Scripture quotations marked (NLT) are taken from the Holy Bible, New Living Translation, copyright © 1996, 2004, 2007 by Tyndale House Foundation. Used by permission of Tyndale House Publishers, Inc., Carol Stream, Illinois 60188. All rights reserved.

Scripture quotations marked (ESV) are taken from the ESV® Bible (The Holy Bible, English Standard Version®), copyright © 2001 by Crossway, a publishing ministry of Good News Publishers. Used by permission. All rights reserved.

Scripture quotations marked (HCSB) are taken from the Holman Christian Standard Bible®, Copyright © 1999, 2000, 2002, 2003, 2009 by Holman Bible Publishers. Used by permission. Holman Christian Standard Bible®, Holman CSB®, and HCSB® are federally registered trademarks of Holman Bible Publishers.

Scripture and/or notes quoted by permission. Quotations designated (NET) are from the NET Bible® copyright ©1996-2016 by Biblical Studies Press, L.L.C. All rights reserved.

Scripture quotations marked (KJV) are taken from the King James Version of the Holy Bible.

For bulk order discounts, please contact Bobby Simpson at bsimpson@friendlycity.net

Library of Congress Control Number: 2023911841
ISBN 978-1-7322358-0-9
Printed in the United States of America

Gratefully Dedicated To
Three Girls And Three Guys

Mary Wright Simpson (Mother) - My mother was an exceptionally unselfish, caring, godly lady who taught me a love for life and a desire to give my all. She was full of energy and enthusiasm that infected those around her. The lessons that she taught me through her words and actions have inspired me to live life fully and to always seek to use God's gifts to share with others.

Bonnie Simpson (Wife) - Bonnie is a truly awesome lady who was strategically placed in my life by God, who knew exactly who I needed. Love is shown in many ways and she has shown me all of those in our 48 years of marriage. There is not enough room here to list all of her qualities, so let me simply say that she is as close as a human can get to being the perfect wife, mother, and grandmother.

Neilie Dunn (Daughter) - My daughter is an inspiration to me. God has richly blessed me, allowing me to share her life as she has grown from a bubbly little girl to a very significant godly businesswoman and civic leader. Along the way, everywhere she has been has become better because she was there. Now, Neilie is the *spitting image* of her mother and grandmothers, a *fantabulous* wife and mother.

Justin Dunn (Son-In-Law) - When you write a dedication, it is really tough for someone to compete with a mother, wife, daughter, and young grandsons. But, when I look at things, Justin helps me weave all of this together. He is a very solid husband for my *little girl* and terrific father for my grandsons. He is patient with my long talks and steady along all our paths. Being a terrific weaver is invaluable.

Cullen Dunn (14-year-old Grandson) - Cullen arrived as an exceptionally awesome gift from God and I could never tell you all that he has done for me and how much he means to me. He is athletic, excels academically, and has an enormously large heart of compassion. In this book, you will learn about his view of my hair and how he taught me to be a *big boy* when I drive over tall bridges.

Ryves Dunn (12-year-old Grandson) - Ryves (pronounced Reeves) loves life and collects friends everywhere he goes. He completely captures my heart and spreads contagious smiles, laughter, and joy along his daily path, while amazing me with the depth of his insight. He got his name from a family member who was chaplain to King Charles I and King Charles II of England. I know that God has fabulous plans for his future.

Almighty God, thank you for strategically placing these people in my life.

THANK YOU SO MUCH!

How in the world can I thank everybody that I should thank? Each of us is a unique accumulation of what God created in us and all the experiences that we have had with thousands of people. As I mention some of you who have been especially helpful with this specific book, I also apologize to others whom I have failed to mention.

First, I want to thank God and my family because I want them to be the core of what I do. God has blessed me in so many ways and allowed me gifts, experiences, and opportunities that made this book possible. I will be eternally grateful to Him.

I mentioned several family members in the Dedication, but I also want to thank each person in my immediate and extended family for their constant love and support throughout the years. Without family, this book would have only been an idea, if even that.

As noted more completely in the Introduction, I am grateful to Dr. David Jeremiah and Dr. Timothy Keller, along with Kevin, Susan, John Thomas, and Josh Belflower. You are the ones who started the final ball rolling.

Much appreciation is due those who read the manuscript, suggesting carefully selected changes, while knowing that I was determined to maintain the originality of the weekly thoughts as much as possible: Tommy and Linda Barber, who also encouraged me many times to write this book; Tami Blackshear, a teaching colleague who always found ways to support this project and caringly guided me to consider ways to improve it while letting it represent who I am; Rachel Willis, a classic, loving lady who continually exudes Christian grace and kindness.

Choosing a title for a book is extremely important and actually took over a year as words were bounced back and forth. I admire the effort, commitment, and love (yes, love) that went into the final eight words. Deep gratitude goes to Kelley Bedrosian, Dr. Tami Blackshear, Dr. Megan Buning, Neilie Dunn, Steve Holmes, and others who contributed to the title.

These days, technology is a huge part of completing a book. Unfortunately, I am only semi-literate in computer skills. But, Dana Spurlin is sensational in that category and she kindly contributed those skills to this project. She spent many hours PATIENTLY putting up with my frequent changes and the other obstacles that I created. Without her help, this book would only be a pile of dusty papers on a bookshelf. Dana, I know that God placed you in the position to make this all come true. Thank you for being the difference maker that I needed. War Eagle!

Scott Beasley, during the development of this book, I bounced a lot of potential covers around in my head. Thankfully, you came on the scene and created "The One" we needed. I will always be grateful for your imagination, patience, wisdom, and kindness.

Christie Leger, you have put up with me for many, many years. You have been much more than an office manager. You have been a true friend and an advisor, a steady rock during many ups and a few downs, and someone off whom I bounced numerous thoughts and ideas. I thank God that He sent you my way.

Steve Holmes, thank you so much for constantly believing in me and graciously answering questions and offering suggestions. You cared and always found time to help. Jim Duggan, you challenged me to consider my legacy and were always asking me about the progress as I wrote. Your sermons, blogs, and conversations have been invaluable. Danny Jones, you have been a major source of godly wisdom in my life. I appreciate you and have learned much from your humble boldness and commitment to truth.

I asked several people to endorse this book and they kindly provided the testimonials that you see for this item. I am deeply indebted to Lawton Bassett, Kelley Bedrosian, Dr. Megan Buning, Mike Candrea, Sheila Cornell Douty, Jim Duggan, Jessica Mendoza, and Dr. Ken Ravizza.

Since 2007, I have written over 800 *Thoughts For Tuesday*. Many readers have kindly sent me encouraging replies or shared these items with a ton of other people. Those messages and actions have been richly appreciated.

To each of you who have been a part of my blessed life journey, I say, "Thank you for all that you have done to insert wisdom and provide joy in my life."

INTRODUCTION

I had major heart surgery (six bypasses) on March 24, 2015 and returned home five days later. I love to read, especially books by Dr. David Jeremiah, and on April 2 began *God Loves You: He always has-He always will*. It was a gift from my niece Susan Belflower, her husband Kevin, and their sons, Josh and John Thomas. I often begin with a book's dedication, acknowledgements, and introduction. The first sixteen words of the acknowledgements in this book literally jumped off the page. Dr. Jeremiah said, "On more than one occasion I have been asked about the process of writing a book." Was God telling *me* to now write the book that a number of people had been encouraging me to do for several years?

I kept pondering those sixteen words for about a week as I completed David Jeremiah's book. The next book that I read was recommended by my friend Tom Draffin and sent to me by my daughter, Neilie, and her family. It was an in-depth look by Timothy Keller at a critical action and entitled, *Prayer: Experiencing Awe and Intimacy with God*. As he wrote about spiritual truth and change, Keller advised readers to ask, "Why might God be showing this to you *today*?" In South Georgia where I live, we would say I got *whopped upside the head* again. I thought back to April 2 and questioned why God had strategically placed those two books and those specific sentences in my hands at the strategic time that He did. My answer to the question regarding strategic placement and timing resulted in this book, *Thoughts For Tuesday: Gold Medal Wisdom For Life*.

Thoughts For Tuesday actually began back in April of 2007 when I decided that a quarterly four-page Higher Ground newsletter was too long and did not communicate often enough. I replaced it with a much shorter, more frequent communication that I promised would be ten or less lines (*Word, Times New Roman*, size 12), followed by scripture and/or a quote that relates to the text. For over sixteen years, I have kept my promise almost without exception. This book basically contains the first 260 of those quick-read items that provide wisdom, instruct, inspire, encourage, and help all of us to Get Better Every Day.

I was determined to keep the messages as close in every way possible to what was distributed on the original dates. The goal was for you to get "reader friendly" items, expressed with words that you know, instead of me trying to impress you with big words. Sometimes, even *made up words* have been used to help you *get the point*. I know a lot about grammar and punctuation, but again chose to prioritize you, the reader. So, I wrote more closely to how we speak than *writing right*. There are very few changes, so you will basically read original items from 2007-2012.

Readers have asked where I keep finding topics. Everywhere! This is a big, big world that God created and there is no limit to His sources for providing wisdom. These lessons may have come from signs on hospital walls, billboards, classrooms, workplaces, really cute and really wise grandsons, friends, life experiences, water bottles, sermons, and a zillion other places. There are a lot of concepts imbedded in wisdom and some may be used more than once, but that's okay. God has given us tons of unique and valuable approaches or illustrations to help us acquire heavenly wisdom.

You can read this book all in one day, read one item each weekday for a year, read it multiple times, or use any other way that fits your personal schedule. Most importantly, consider *wearing this book*. Interact with it. When I read books, I write like crazy in them. I underline, highlight, star, circle words, draw arrows, and make a *boocoodle* (lots) of notes. This is YOUR book, so I encourage you to do more than just read it. Figure out how you can apply it and then actually do apply it. Let it help you improve your life and please share timely *Thoughts* to help others.

I have been diligent, but I must admit that human ability to acquire and share wisdom is limited. The best source of true wisdom comes from our Heavenly Father. *"For My thoughts are not your thoughts, Nor are your ways My ways," says the* LORD. *"For as the heavens are higher than the earth, So are My ways higher than your ways, And My thoughts than your thoughts."* Isaiah 55:8-9 NKJV

I stated earlier that God strategically timed and placed two catalytic sentences in my personal path. I hope that each of you will find items that come straight from these pages right when you need them most. I have thoroughly enjoyed writing this book and I pray that you will thoroughly enjoy using it.

THOUGHTS FOR TUESDAY
GOLD MEDAL WISDOM FOR LIFE

2007

*The fear of the Lord is the beginning of **wisdom**; A good understanding have all those who do His commandments. His praise endures forever (emphasis added). Psalm 111:10 NKJV*

Tuesday - April 17, 2007

For about 15 years, I conducted a Monday through Friday five-minute radio program during which I reported on local sports in Tifton, Georgia. To spice it up a little, I added some extras like (1) "What Happened In Sports On This Date" in some past year, (2) interviews with local sports figures, and (3) "A Thought For Tuesday" on each Tuesday morning. I love finding and sharing little **nuggets** and often place those in our regular newsletter. As you well know, most of the time I elaborate and expand that thought into paragraphs or pages. Today, I am starting a regular Higher Ground email similar to what I did on the radio program. My promise is that it will ALWAYS be ten or less lines…a quick moment or item to just make all of us think. I may just give you a thought, I may share an idea, or I may mention one of our activities or products in <11 lines.

Let the words of my mouth and the meditation of my heart Be acceptable in Your sight, O LORD, my strength and my Redeemer. Psalm19:14 NKJV

Tuesday - April 24, 2007

When I reduced my international softball activities three years ago and began to teach at the local high school, in addition to regular Higher Ground activities, I was simply amazed at how many young people used built-in excuses consisting of 3-4 letters and/or numbers. While many were accurate, based on evaluations, many used it as an excuse. Others developed their own excuses. I often have said that losers make excuses and winners make results. Raymond Berry, NFL Hall of Fame receiver, had a weak back, one leg shorter than another, and poor vision. Michael Phelps is ADHD and won six Gold Medals in the 2004 Olympics. Pete Rose, career leader for MLB hits, was not drafted. Gold Medal gymnast Mary Lou Retton had to practice starting at six each morning. Dave Thomas, founder of Wendy's, did not know his birthplace or parents. These people refused to let LOE (Lack Of Effort) stop them. Their **work ethic** led them to success.

If I had not come and spoken to them, they would have no sin, but now they have no excuse for their sin. John 15:22 NKJV

Tuesday - May 1, 2007

Rarely does a day go by that we do not see or hear numbers that compare someone to someone else. It may be in softball, where we see a list of team or individual statistics, like team records of wins and losses, or batting averages or ERA's listed in order, ranking individuals in comparison to others. It could be school grades that compare a person's grade to some standard scale that gives them an A, B, C, or F. It may even be "pass or fail" on a standard test, like some in Georgia where getting 47 percent right is all that's needed to pass. Some of this comparison to others or to standards developed by others can be okay, but be careful. The most **effective measures** compare someone to what they are capable of, not to what someone else does.

Each one should test his own actions. Then he can take pride in himself, without comparing himself to somebody else, for each one should carry his own load. Galatians 6:4-5 NIV

Tuesday - May 8, 2007

Far too many high school students end up with a grade below 70, or some other passing standard. The word *failure* is used to describe that grade. Some educational gurus say the teacher fails to teach, but my observation is that the student usually fails to do what is necessary to pass. In athletics, we also talk a lot about failure. Often, we incorrectly define failure by the result; like the person who hits .300 being said to fail 7 times out of 10. I strongly disagree, since the hitter does not have total control of what a hit is. A bullet line drive caught by the shortstop should not be classified a failure. Point To Remember - Brent Strom, very insightful former MLB coach, says two things can happen when the pitcher throws the ball, and both are good…it does what he wants or he learns something. **Failure** can be successful IF used to push us to success.

Whenever you fall, pick up something. Oswald Theodore Avery

Tuesday - May 15, 2007

Incremental improvement or quantum leap…which is it that we should be seeking in sports and in life? In our full-length newsletters, I have mentioned the Japanese word *kaizen* several times, reminding all of us of their corporate approach to *continuous improvement*. That is certainly what we need at times, a determined journey of perseverance that gets us there a little bit at a time. At other times, the immediate improvement or quantum leap is needed and perhaps possible. So, do we *Get Better Every Day or* do we get better overnight? I guess there is some of each and the best in their field maybe figure out more often which is the **best approach** for the situation. I recently saw a nugget that perhaps says all of this pretty accurately, a rhyme of words that seems to state the goal better than I'd seen it before.

Good, better, best – never let it rest – till your good is better and your better best. John Furphy

Tuesday - May 22, 2007

I think it was a little over ten years ago that I met a lady who impressed me with an almost constant smile. Judi Garman had asked me to speak at her annual clinic at Cal State Fullerton and one of her assistant coaches was Michelle Gromacki. She was a fine instructor and has since become the Head Coach at CSF and spent several years as part of the USA National Team staff. Anyway, her smile was energizing. Since I often seek to increase energy levels and decrease energy leaks, I thought it would be nice to remind all of us today about the power of a smile. Realize just how helpful it is to smile. The light of a powerful **smile** can rev up energy, decrease conflict, lighten the stress level, and increase performance. Just watch the results.

When I smiled at them, they scarcely believed it; the light of my face was precious to them. Job 29:24 NIV

Tuesday - May 29, 2007

I am amazed how **words** are used to *impress* rather than *express*. Educators are taught to use *collaborative pairs*, which really just means two people working together, or partners. Information is called *peripheral*, which basically just means it's useless. Many teachers are required to develop *essential questions* for each lesson and/or unit, when all that means is to tell people what the lesson is about, but put in the less understandable form of a question. I always figured if they paid attention, they would know what the lesson is about. And, if the teachers fail to use *differentiated instruction* (use different methods for different people) well enough, they might get *terminated* (used to be they got fired). Today, stop trying to impress people with big words that few really understand. When you really want to be understood, say things simply.

Words are conversational terrorism. Brent Strom, Major League Baseball Coach

Tuesday - June 5, 2007

Bill Laxton, a friend from Newmarket, Ontario, recently watched his daughter Carly, a former member of our Higher Ground International Player Advisory Board, graduate from Northwood University in Michigan. He shared a thought from the commencement speaker, O. Temple Sloan, Jr., and suggested that I share it with you. I will now do so. "There is no right way to do the wrong thing." That is simple and powerful, and we should daily consider its merits. A few days later, a sister-in-law gave me a copy of a fairly recent issue of *Reader's Digest* and it contained a related thought from Peter Drucker, an icon (that means a very respected, well known guru) in the world of business management. He wisely stated that "Management is doing things right; leadership is doing **the right things**." Chew on those two thoughts, apply where appropriate, and have a terrific Tuesday.

This is what the Lord says: "Maintain justice and do what is right, for my salvation is close at hand and my righteousness will soon be revealed."
Isaiah 56:1 NIV

Tuesday - June 12, 2007

In early 2001, I was part of a staff that developed the plan for the inaugural Greek National Softball Team. We then selected and coached them in their first international competition and 2001 European Championship Tournament. It was an extremely rewarding experience to help start a softball program in a country that did not have softball. It was definitely a challenge to develop athletes from track, swimming, and gymnastics and help them learn rules and skills of a strange new sport. It was likewise a challenge to educate federation leaders about team selection, skill development, and strategy. It was a mixture of challenge, frustration, emotional fatigue, and pure joy as wonderful ladies gave so much of themselves and made huge progress. On a training and game trip to Holland, Head Coach Craig Montvidas had his six-year-old son address the team before a game. His short message allowed us to focus on **the core** of our project and is terrific advice today as we continue to seek excellence.

Just have fun! Quinn Montvidas

Tuesday - June 19, 2007

I really enjoy working with dedicated softball players. It's just pure fun to watch their approach and how they prepare in practice and perform in games. One of the nicest things is to see two such players working together and creating a human equation where one plus one is greater than two. At summer camps, I frequently tell players to be very careful who they choose as their partner for drills. I tell them that their mama is right…**it really does matter who you hang around with**. Pick friends and training partners (not necessarily the same) wisely. We can debate parts of the old saying below (attributed to various sources), but it contains some good advice.

He who knows not and knows not that he knows not, he is a fool; avoid him.
He who knows not and knows that he knows not, he is simple; teach him.
He who knows and knows not that he knows, he is asleep; wake him.
He who knows and knows that he knows, he is wise; follow him.

Tuesday - June 26, 2007

It always inspires me when I hear an interview with military personnel in combat areas. Almost without fail, they shift every question into a very focused area. Whether it is a veteran officer or a young person who just arrived, they emphasize the word **mission**. They use what Laurie Beth Jones calls *planned abandonment*. They consciously avoid a broad light bulb view and instead place **laser beam focus** on their mission. They conquer distractions with this *zoomed in* focus on mission. They ask themselves "What is my mission" and then they do all within their power to accomplish it. For us to be successful in a hitting drill, a pitching workout, designing a practice, or living our life, we must first establish the core mission. We must have a central purpose. Anything else is just a *blowing in the wind* approach and it's rarely successful.

Practice "planned abandonment" of opportunities that would merely serve as distractions. Laurie Beth Jones, author of *Jesus, Life Coach*

Tuesday - July 3, 2007

A couple of weeks ago, we discussed the importance of hanging around the right people. Today, when I recalled that item, it also made me recall a related subject that I had discussed about 8-10 years ago in our newsletter. A *Reader's Digest* story quoted Ben Carson saying, "Go down to the fish market and look into the crab barrel. They never have to put a lid on it because if one crab starts to crawl out, the others will grab on to him and pull him back down. That's what negative peer pressure does." Our daily mission should be to avoid being impacted by the **crabs** that want to pull us down to their standard. Instead, we should determine to be a lifter who pulls others up and we must stay very close to other **lifters** who reach down and pull us up. What about you? Do you pull others back into the barrel of sameness and mediocrity or do you help pull them up to higher ground?

I will extol You, O Lord, for You have lifted me up, And have not let my foes rejoice over me. Psalm 30:1 NKJV

Tuesday - July 10, 2007

Do you know how many seconds are in day? It's 86,400 (24x60x60). **Time** is one resource with which I am more than a little obsessed. I take routes in my small town based on the number of traffic lights and the color I see when I look at them from blocks away. I drive my wife nuts using the TV remote to watch several programs at a time. One of my pet peeves is that so many people arrive late to clinics, making it very difficult to get started effectively. Well, a few days ago, I spent three days in a truly wonderful place with fantastic people doing a clinic for players and coaches. The first morning's instruction started at 8:00 and everyone was checked in and ready to go by 7:50. That just does not happen very many places. I was immediately infatuated with the people of Bethel, Maine, and by the end of the clinic, I was deeply in love. In the future, I'll share more about that clinic. For now, work to *Bethelize* your life.

The way you manage your time reflects what's really important to you.
Bob Briner

Tuesday - July 17, 2007

I often ask people the following question. "If five frogs were sitting on a log, and three decided to jump off, how many would be left on the log." The typical answer, using very basic arithmetic, is two. Of course, I then get to tell them that they are wrong. Three frogs deciding to jump off does not necessarily mean that they actually did jump off. Many times, we decide but don't do. Hitters decide to swing at a pitch, but the bat does not move. Or, they decide to not swing and the bat somehow just swings itself. We have to realize that deciding and doing are not always the same.

To actually do what we decide takes purpose, passion, deep intent, and superb commitment. It also takes a lot of repetition under game conditions. Commit today to first make better decisions and, second, to follow through and **act on the decision**. Get off the log.

If you start to take Vienna, take Vienna. Napoleon Bonaparte

Tuesday - July 24, 2007

Amy Jackson, who has come all the way from Alaska with her daughter Cory to attend several of our camps in Georgia, recently sent an email that ended with *Taikuu,* which means **Thank You** in the Inupiac language. This is a perfect time to say *Taikuu* to coaches, players, parents, and facility personnel who made our summer camps successful. Also, let me say *Taikuu* to all of you who have supported Higher Ground and encouraged us to help others *Get Better Every Day*. By the way, **Thank You** is the proper reply when someone compliments you. It helps build confidence. The response some people use when receiving a compliment is to say they were lucky or something similar. Actually, that tells the *complementor* (my word) that they lied. Just say **Thank You** and add the positive comment to your confidence account. It also works well when you receive criticism…it can diffuse or even create closure for an explosive situation.

Enter his gates with thanksgiving and his courts with praise; give thanks to him and praise his name. Psalm 100:4 NIV

Tuesday - July 31, 2007

I was in a meeting recently when the concept of *job description* came up. I always remember that many job descriptions used when I was in local government seemed to end with the statement "**Other duties as assigned**." Wouldn't it be nice if we all realized that our "job" is often to do whatever is morally correct to get the right result for the team or organization to which we belong? Then, we would understand the value of the role we play, the sacrifice bunt that is signaled, and our place in the batting order or organizational chart. Maybe, we would not gripe so much when we do not get everything we want. We would better understand that we get to do some pleasurable tasks and then sometimes we get to do some that are not so pleasant. It's kinda like eating…mama says we get to eat some fried chicken, steak, shrimp, or other things we like, but she also makes us eat the carrots, broccoli, stewed okra, or whatever we do not like.

If you are too big to do little things then you are too little to do big things.

Tuesday - August 7, 2007

I study **how people respond** to things. Take the concept of *age*. When a sweet young lady turns thirteen, people start to say she's a crazy teenager. Actually, she is just a sweet young lady who is one day older than the day before. When the coach turns 50 or 60, people suddenly call him old and want to send him to the Double S Ranch for senility and slowness. My wife, Bonnie, recently showed me a saying in the 1975 Mayfield, Kentucky *Junior League Cookbook* (my mother grew up there). It said "The same rain that grows weeds for the pessimist, sprinkles flowers for the optimist." Like our response to age, we choose how we respond to rain, an umpire's call, or a coach's decision to bat us eighth. This principle is also very true in sports and daily life. We can choose weeds or flowers. Determine today to choose better responses and you will have chosen a path that greatly increases the odds for achieving joy and success.

The same fire that melts the butter hardens the egg. Anonymous quote from a college class

Tuesday - August 14, 2007

I have spent a lot of time with Greg Riddoch, former manager of the San Diego Padres. During camps, clinics, filming videos, phone calls, and lots of highway miles, we have shared many thoughts. As two very talkative friends, we have missed a lot of turnoffs because we were focused on our sharing instead of our driving. That's okay…it gave us longer to share. One of the first things I learned from him was to **ask better questions**. So often, we ask a group to repeat what we said or to give an answer. If we get the right reply (often from the same person or small sub-group), we incorrectly think the entire group understands. We also ask far too many Yes or No questions. A monkey guessing can get half of those correct. Management guru Peter Drucker said, "The leader of the future will be a person who knows how to ask." That's also true for the leader of today, so improve your asking and use more higher-level questioning.

Ask, and it will be given to you; seek, and you will find; knock, and it will be opened to you. Matthew 7:7 NKJV

Tuesday - August 21, 2007

In a book sent to me by my daughter's boss, I read about a bird in a shell. We know that a bird must leave the shell so it can grow stronger, learn to fly, and live a normal life. It seems it would be kind of us to help the bird get out of its shell so it could start to enjoy real life. If we found a bird captured in its shell, we might kindly crack the shell so it would not have to struggle so hard to escape the tough prison. We would consider ourselves being a compassionate *shell breaker* and *bird releaser*. In reality, we would be conducting a very cruel act. The bird needs **time to struggle** with the shell. If not, it leaves in a weakened condition and will soon be unable to deal with other items in its environment. Because the bird has not been allowed to strengthen through struggle, it will have little ability to cope with what otherwise would be manageable. Learning to struggle can often bring strength. Be kind and allow others the freedom to struggle.

If we are not allowed to deal with small problems, we will be destroyed by slightly larger ones. Jim Stovall in *The Ultimate Gift*

Tuesday - August 28, 2007

As an instructor, I am often asked to help solve a problem. It may be while working with a parent or coach trying to help a child or player, an athlete suffering through a time of poor performance, or an Algebra student who thinks they cannot work a problem. All of us **search for solutions**. We need principles to follow so that we increase the odds for successful results. Unfortunately, we often just try to apply more time, money, and effort and think that will solve the problems. Numerous examples in sports, public education, government, relationships and other areas of life show that these may be valuable, but far too often are not solutions. It is critical to first properly plan and prepare. Be willing to do the up-front, philosophical work and effectively apply the thought below. Study each individual specific situation with insight and apply a proper solution. Otherwise, you are misusing the time, money, and effort.

Flawless execution cannot compensate for implementing the wrong solution. Daryl Conner, quoted in *The Performance Edge*, by Robert K. Cooper

Tuesday - September 4, 2007

Most of you don't know Judith Gibson. She is a lady at my church in a town most of you don't know called Ty Ty, Georgia. She is an *Encourager* and she sent me a couple of thoughts (see one below) on June 29. In our school, we are having educational gurus try to pound into us that "failure is not an option." Like many clichés, that one is a myth or at the least, it's a partial-truth. The bird that I mentioned two weeks ago must fail many times as it attempts to break its shell. A softball hitter must likewise face failure and learn from it while journeying to higher levels, as must the aspiring pitcher, pianist, dancer, parent, corporate leader, or inventor (Thomas Edison and the light bulb). **Failure MUST be an option** if anyone is to accept the challenge to grow, improve, and accomplish great things. You must be willing to slog through the deep, frustrating, and exhilarating mud of failure as you move to the solid, green turf of success.

Far better it is to dare mighty things, to win glorious triumphs, even though checkered by failure, than to rank with those poor spirits who neither enjoy nor suffer much, because they live in a gray twilight that knows not victory nor defeat. Theodore Roosevelt

Tuesday - September 11, 2007

Last week, I shared something that Judith Gibson passed along from Theodore Roosevelt. This week, consider something that Lilly Rossetti recently shared. You may not know her. She is a very fine Italian who recently coached the Spanish Women's National Softball Team to the European B Championship. She has been my translator in Italy and Germany, an instructor at our clinics and camps, and is a wonderful friend. She shared this simple item that appeared in a newsletter from Tom Hanson, co-author of *Heads Up Baseball* with Ken Ravizza, "…a woman (was) cooking with a bunch of peas. As she was pouring them from a bowl to a pot, one bounced away and landed on the floor. She picked it up. Put it in the sink. And kept working. That's it. That's the whole story. Not much to it, but **THAT'S THE POINT**. No drama. No big reaction. No scheming on how to put off dealing with it. Pick it up. Deal with it. Move on."

When Jesus had finished these parables, he moved on from there.
Matthew 13:53 NIV

Tuesday - September 18, 2007

Often, I hear athletes, students, and many others use four-letter words. Many are profane, obscene, and disgusting, but one of the most damaging is the contraction for cannot. How many times a day do we hear others, or ourselves, use the word **can't**? We face a challenge to make a change in athletic mechanics, or need to change our way of thinking, receive a request to employ a new approach, or simply should solve some problem in life. Some things should not be done, but for the things that need to be done, our reply is often, "I can't do that." Most of the time, people compare where they are with where they are asked to go or what they know with what they need to know. Since they feel unqualified using where they are to get where they need to be, they bail out with "I can't." They try to use *here* to predict *there* or the *present* to predict the *future*. Nido Qubein and all of us really know better. Start here so **you can get there**.

Your present circumstances don't determine where you can go; they merely determine where you start. Nido Qubein

Tuesday - September 25, 2007

I teach Algebra, so I spend a lot of time dealing with equations, discussing one thing that equals another. Today, I'd like for you to consider some **inequalities**, where things do not equal what many think they do. Some are quotes and some are my thoughts. I'll have more for you soon. Disagreement does not equal disrespect (U.S. Army Retired General Gordon Sullivan)…Unity does not equal uniformity (Rick Warren)… Walking *hand in hand* does not equal seeing *eye to eye* (Rick Warren)… Having a failure does not equal being a failure…Speed on a radar gun does not equal good pitching…Great mechanics do not equal great hitting…A great arm does not equal great throwing…Great speed does not equal great baserunning…A proper decision does not equal a proper action…Money does not equal success…Winning games does not equal great coaching…Knowledge does not equal wisdom…Skill does not equal achievement.

Have this mind among yourselves, which is yours in Christ Jesus, who, though he was in the form of God, did not count equality with God a thing to be grasped, but emptied himself, by taking the form of a servant, being born in the likeness of men. Philippians 2:5-7 ESV

Tuesday - October 2, 2007

Sport psychologists often use the term *visualization*, basically a fancy 13-letter word for what we see in our mind, or "in our mind's eye." It's really what I'd call *sensization*, since we should do our best to not only see it, but to add other senses so we often hear it, feel it, taste it, and smell it in our mind. Before the actual action, a hitter should strive to see, hear, and feel the ball exploding off her bat and landing in an unreachable area. A student should see himself getting a paper back with a large A, the salesman should see the contract being signed, and the project manager should see the beautiful finished structure. Prior practice of mental *sensization* will not guarantee it, but will increase the odds of physical success. In the 1984 Olympics, 16 year-old gymnast Mary Lou Retton needed a perfect 10 to win the all-around gold. Just before her final event, she flashed her magic smile at a TV camera and 80 million viewers. Later asked what she had been thinking, she replied, "I was thinking. Watch this. I'm going to do it."

Those who see the invisible can do the impossible. Carl Mays

Tuesday - October 9, 2007

Through Higher Ground, I provide softball instructional services and products. I also teach high school Algebra. Softball players and high school math students often get distracted. I work to help them recognize and conquer their **distractions**. I am convinced that all of us…players, coaches, students, and teachers…often misunderstand distractions. A little over a year ago, I sat near Sarah Beth Merritt in church. She is a fine young lady who made an A in my Algebra 2 class, and she is also a skilled soccer player at our school. While she was "twirling twigs" in her hair, I noticed that she was intently focused on the pastor or her Bible. As soon as she stopped "twirling twigs," and either scratched her head or pulled a hair out, it was obvious that she lost focus. Scratching and pulling were distractions, but the similar action of twirling was not. How often do we tell someone to stop something that may actually be helping their focus?

I need a distraction so that I can focus. Student Sara McStott

Tuesday - October 16, 2007

In November 2000, the ISF sent me to Greece to help develop a plan that would culminate with a host team for the 2004 Olympics in Athens. It was a country that had no softball, so it was a difficult and rewarding challenge. Eight months later, Craig Montvidas, Cindy Bristow, and I took fourteen fine ladies to the European B Championships. They were barely beginners, but they were ready to give their very best. Below are some of their **expectations** just before the event. Pardon the spelling…cherish the insight.

* Begin to trust each other…understand each other with one glance and finally come together like ONE* Want to be strong if things get ruff and pass this on to all the team!!* Be by far the team with the greatest enthusiasm and willingness to learn and absorb whatever happens* To have fun, to live the experience and learn from this*Play as well as I can (at the moment)*I expect us to surprise many people and this because we are VERY EXCITED! And will put all our HEART on the FEILD!!!*

as it is my eager expectation and hope that I will not be at all ashamed, but that with full courage now as always Christ will be honored in my body, whether by life or by death. Philippians 1:20 ESV

Tuesday - October 23, 2007

Today's society is quick to label things, and people are one of those things. We hear labels like no power, slow bat, poor velocity, too slow, can't throw, bad hands, too short, slow learner, not good at this or that, small business, bad location. Education and psychologists may label students as ADD, ADHD, or SST. The problem with these labels, even if accurate, is that people absorb them and allow them to over-control their achievements, or lack of achievements. Labels become controllers, instead of challenges. Many people arrive at the "obstacle wall" and get a dose of DNC (*Do Not Care*) or LOE (*Lack of Effort*), thereby eliminating any possible success that could result from proper thought, innovation, superb effort, or just pure guts. I see it daily on the field and in the classroom. The label becomes the excuse. The cure for *labelitis* is often just taking multiple ***gotta wanna*** injections and just plain old **hanging in there** until you get it done.

*If you **gotta wanna** bad enough, then you'll figure out how to do it* (emphasis added). Tom Peters, *The Pursuit of WOW!*

Tuesday - October 30, 2007

Our interim pastor told a terrific story a week ago and I want to share it with you because it applies to softball, baseball, other sports, business, math classes, and life in general. He said that a little black boy in the western part of Africa gave a very beautiful shell to a missionary as an offering. Knowing that the shell came from a beach quite far from the village, the missionary said "You had to walk 15-20 miles roundtrip to the beach site to get this shell. That's a very long walk," The little boy replied, "**Long walk part of gift**." Too often, we want to get something valuable and not pay the price. We want "something for nothing." We want the free lunch, the magic pill, the drive-through, microwave, *zappable* success. We must realize that success normally comes from a sacrificial, long-walk journey and not from some *instantized* magic. Part of the talent or so-called gift that we see in skilled performance is the long walk to get there.

But if we hope for what we do not see, we eagerly wait for it with perseverance. Romans 8:25 NKJV

Tuesday - November 6, 2007

Many years ago, when I coached baseball at Florida State, the first baseman was Jim Foxwell, a quick-witted young man from New Jersey. Other players would often do their best to ask Jim questions that would stump him, but rarely did they succeed. I remember clearly the question asked of Jim one day on a bus ride to a game, "Jim, how many grains of sand are on the beach?" Quicker than the Lone Ranger's speeding bullet, Jim asked back, "High tide or low tide?" In his small question is a big message. Before we jump to a poor conclusion, a foot is inserted in the mouth, or an incorrect action is taken, let's take whatever time is available to get **complete, accurate, necessary information**. This will help us swing at better pitches, hold the ball when no play is possible, build better mousetraps, strengthen teams, and simply live a much more joyful life. Okay?

He had been instructed in the way of the Lord, and he spoke with great fervor and taught about Jesus accurately, though he knew only the baptism of John. He began to speak boldly in the synagogue. When Priscilla and Aquila heard him, they invited him to their home and explained to him the way of God more adequately. Acts 18:25-26 NIV

Tuesday - November 13, 2007

I am about to read a book by Erik Weihenmayer, co-authored by Paul G. Stoltz. A friend named Dalton Ruer gave it to me in Dalton, Georgia (The double-Dalton is just a coincidence). It's about Erik, a man who has reached each of the Seven Summits, the tallest peak in each continent. I am totally absorbed in achieving excellence and climbing to higher ground as we seek to *Get Better Every Day*. At the same time, I have a fear of any open height higher than the second level of a typical stepladder. To even think of climbing a mountain makes my hands and feet sweat from fear. I have great respect for anyone who can train so well and **overcom**e all the **obstacles** involved in scaling the heights of these mountains, so I am writing about it even before I read the book. I forgot to tell you the title is *The Adversity Advantage: Turning Everyday Struggles Into Everyday Greatness*. Oops, I also forgot to tell you that Erik, the climber, is blind.

Kites rise highest against the wind, not with it. Sir Winston Churchill

Tuesday - November 20, 2007

When I conduct softball instruction, math instruction, or life instruction, I often discuss an acronym that involves the letter *A* being used twice. In my explanation, each *A* represents the word *ASK* because I want to double-emphasize the importance of the learner asking questions. At a softball clinic in Colorado, I once asked a group of young ladies what they thought the second *A* might stand for. An insightful teenage girl named Katie Fear suggested the word ***ADJUST***. I was looking for the word ***ASK***, but she provided the word ***ADJUST***. You know, that is really why we should ***ASK***…so we can learn and ***ADJUST***! Because I decided to ***ASK***, I am now able to ***ADJUST***, add a third *A* to my acronym, and have a better way to provide a critical principle of instruction. Remember to *ASK* and *ADJUST*, and you too can increase the odds of making all *A's* in softball, math, or life.

And he said: "Truly I tell you, unless you change and become like little children, you will never enter the kingdom of heaven." Matthew 18:3 NIV

Tuesday - November 27, 2007

About a year ago, my brother-in-law, Jimmy Spurlin, passed away. Through his volunteer work as a coach (many sports; won several ASA Nationals coaching boys softball) and umpire, he had a profound effect on many young men and women. Dr. Greg Anderson, one of his former players and a pallbearer at the funeral, wrote to the local newspaper, "Philanthropy comes in many different forms, but **what greater gift** can a man give than spending his **valuable time teaching kids**…If he had invested his time and directed his passion into making money, he would have died a much wealthier man. I bet, if given the opportunity, he wouldn't change a thing. Thanks, Coach." How are you investing your time? In sports or in life, do you have the right impact on others? All of us, regardless of our age or position, have wonderful opportunities to invest our time wisely, to impact others powerfully. What greater gift can we give? Invest well!!

*Learn to estimate a person's importance not by income, but by output * No man stood so straight as when he stooped to help a child * Children are today's investment and tomorrow's dividend.

Tuesday - December 4, 2007

Recently, the traffic on I-95 was the old *stop-and-go*. We would go 60-70 mph, then quickly stop and creep, then repeat the process, requiring steady focus ahead to prevent rear-ending someone. BUT, I remembered reading an article that said a driver who stops quickly should **check the rearview mirror** to ensure that trailing cars do not rear end him. A driver must focus on what's ahead, but also know where he is and check what's behind him. If we spend too much time in the rearview mirror, we end up in a ditch or attached to someone's rear bumper, but it's vital to see what's behind us. Many helpers, whether certified or self-appointed, tell us to forget the past and surge into the future. This **traffic analogy** provides a better strategy. Maybe we ought to spend a lot of our time working toward the future. But, while fully aware of our present, we must also effectively use what's behind us to properly guide us from where we are to where we need to be.

The windshield is bigger than the rearview mirror, but both are critical to success.

Tuesday - December 11, 2007

Hitting a baseball or softball is a very **complex task**. The whole action from release of ball to bat meeting ball only takes about 0.4 seconds. The hitter must see it, figure out what is seen, decide what to do, and do it. That's a lot to do in a short period of time, when you realize that just taking a step involves well over 100 bones, muscles, tendons, and ligaments. Many other tasks in our life are also complex. The job of an instructor or a performer is to **simplify it**. Can you shrink the complexity of hitting to just "see it and rip it?" Likewise, simplify adult visualization to a child pretending or conflict resolution to a sincere smile? Can you condense teamwork to one soldier having only the weapon and another just having the bullets, or the complexity of solving life's problems to using *what you have* to get *what you need*? Jack Stallings taught me long ago that "the more complex the skill, the more simple must be our explanation." What about yours? Is it simple?

Out of clutter, find Simplicity. From discord, find Harmony. In the middle of difficulty lies Opportunity. Albert Einstein

Tuesday - December 18, 2007

Three days ago, my daughter, Neilie, and her husband, Justin, gave me a copy of Charles Stanley's book *Living The Extraordinary Life*. He begins the introduction with, "On April 12, 1945, President Franklin Delano Roosevelt was at the Little White House in Warm Springs, Georgia, sitting for a portrait, when he died suddenly of a cerebral hemorrhage." Stanley went on to say that the artist, Elizabeth Shoumatoff, never fully completed the work and it has since been called the *Unfinished Portrait*. I got to thinking that the most important works that we do in athletics and in life should also be **unfinished portraits**. The work done by the instructor, player, or student learning or improving softball skills, life skills, or mastering a dance should never be finished. Neither should developing a concept, conducting business, raising a family, or structuring a relationship. Never satisfied, we should strive to *Get Better Every Day* in our quest for excellence.

Now our knowledge is partial and incomplete, and even the gift of prophecy reveals only part of the whole picture! 1 Corinthians 13:9 NLT

Tuesday - December 25, 2007

When we recently studied the CHRISTmas story at our church, Peggy Crumley made a statement that we should always remember that the wise men were **seeking** Jesus. On that day, that word landed solid and stuck in my mind. In our lives, whether in our Christian walk, athletics, business, education, or personal relationships, we should be *seekers*. Of course, we should seek the right things and then give our best, just like the wise men gave gold, frankincense, and myrrh. I once read a statement by Major League Baseball manager Joe Maddon, who earlier in his career was a fine hitting coach, teaching that a hitter should "*hunt* his pitch" early in the count. The same is actually true late in the count…the definition of "his pitch" just changes to include more locations. Let's all improve our ability to hunt, search, and seek. Identify the best things to seek and then give your best to those best things. The wise men set a good example to follow.

Now after Jesus was born in Bethlehem of Judea in the days of Herod the king, behold, wise men from the East came to Jerusalem, saying, "Where is He who has been born King of the Jews? For we have seen His star in the East and have come to worship Him." Matthew 2:1-2 NKJV

THOUGHTS FOR TUESDAY
GOLD MEDAL WISDOM FOR LIFE

2008

Who is **wise** and understanding among you? Let him show by good conduct that his works are done in the meekness of **wisdom** (emphasis added). James 3:13 NKJV

Tuesday - January 1, 2008

In 1898, Johnson Oatman, Jr. wrote a hymn called "Higher Ground." If you did not already know, you likely figured out as you read the last sentence that this is where the name of our business came from. Actually, the corporate name is Getting Better Every Day, Inc., dba/Higher Ground. Oatman penned, *"I'm pressing on the upward way, New heights I'm gaining every day; Still praying as I onward bound, 'Lord, plant my feet on higher ground.' Lord, lift me up and let me stand, By faith, on heaven's tableland, A higher plane than I have found; Lord, plant my feet on higher ground."* People make resolutions this time of year, promising as Ann Grubbs said in our Sunday School class to "improve something." They vow to lose weight, stop smoking, be nicer, exercise more, stop a bad habit, or start a good one. Let's all vow to "**press on the upward way**" and have our feet on higher ground on January 1, 2009, than they are today on January 1, 2008.

The biggest room in the world is the room for improvement. H. Schmidt

Tuesday - January 8, 2008

In our quest to improve, to *Get Better Every Day*, we must do more than hope to get better. One of my all-time favorite books, *Hope Is Not A Method*, written by former Army Chief of Staff Gordon R Sullivan and Michael V. Harper, provides useful insight on change. Warning us of jumping too quickly into the physical work of improvement, they write, "The most important phase…is **the front-end work** – the in-depth, serious thinking – that results in the intellectual framework for the future. Imaging the future first takes place in the mind…this intellectual change guides the physical changes – in process, structure, and output…Without the tough up-front work of intellectual change, physical change will be unfocused, random, and unlikely to succeed…Change must occur first in people's minds; only then can it take place in the structure, processes, performance, and output." What about you…what comes first, mental or physical?

Before you move bricks and mortar, you must move your mind. Sullivan & Harper

Tuesday - January 15, 2008

We live in a world of phrases and slogans. We are bombarded by catchy little word combinations in sports, business, education, and especially now in the season of political speeches. Many of them are empty, but some are very helpful. One of my favorites came from a former USA Olympic Team and we can apply it to our personal situations. Their slogan was **"*in spite of.*"** They decided that they would win the Gold Medal *in spite of* whatever might happen. They chose to win *in spite of* injuries, player drama, coaching mistakes, administrative issues, bad calls by officials, travel, weather, and other obstacles. Likewise, we can choose to achieve excellence *in spite of* the obstacles we face…not enough time, fatigue, a grouchy boss, insane efforts to clone us and stifle creative excellence, poor leadership, not enough money, players with less skill, bad bounces, unfair decisions, or steep climbs. They won Gold **in spite of**. Will we?

Obstacles don't have to stop you. If you run into a wall, don't turn around and give up. Figure out how to climb it, go through it, or work around it. Michael Jordan

Tuesday - January 22, 2008

In November 1998, Craig Montvidas, the very insightful Head Coach of the Dutch National Team, sent a large number of his players to five USA coaches for a week of specialized training. Five infielders came here for me to assist with hitting and infield play. One day, we spent some leisure time allowing them to ride horses with my brother-in-law. Several had never ridden a horse, so the group began by slowly walking the horses around a pond. Without warning, Marjan Smit's horse became startled and began a rapid gallop through some small pine trees, with Marjan screaming. When Tommy finally reached her and stopped the horse, he asked her why she had not just told the horse to STOP. Shaken, she said "I told him STOP in four different languages, but he would not stop." If we expect someone to hear and act, we must remember to **communicate in the language of the listener**, even if we have to try more than four ways.

You can have brilliant ideas, but if you can't get them across, your ideas won't get you anywhere. Lee Iacocca

Tuesday - January 29, 2008

As a teenage baseball player, I would always say **"My fault"** when I'd make bad throws or other mistakes. That is, until Benny Dees coached my summer team. Tired of that, he quickly told me in no uncertain terms that he knew it was my fault and that he'd run my guts out if he heard it again. I learned to keep my mouth shut and work hard and smart to do things right more often. Today, when I tell students to quit talking in class, they often say **"Sorry."** I tell them that I do not want them to just be sorry, but that I want them to change their behavior. I also get bugged by frequent school announcements that begin, **"Please excuse** this interruption…" Don't constantly ask me to excuse them. Instead, respect classroom instructional time and find better times and methods for communication. Likewise, this principle applies to frequently being late, being rude, or having a messy room. The **best apologies** are wrapped in better actions.

Right actions in the future are the best apologies for bad actions in the past. Tryon Edwards - Theologian & Author (1809-1894)

Tuesday - February 5, 2008

Remember Erik Weihenmayer, the blind man that climbed the highest mountain on each continent? In his books on adversity, he discusses three types of **responses to challenges**. He notes that *Quitters* simply give up. The *Campers* work hard, apply themselves, and push to a pretty high position, then settle for that level of comfort. His research of about 150,000 corporate leaders indicates that a large majority of people fit one of these two categories. A few people are *Climbers.* People in this very small remnant "continue to learn, grow, strive, and improve until their final breath." His research indicates that the difference is in how they respond to adversity. They do more than cope…they actually *use adversity* and unleash tremendous energy, innovation, and momentum. They push beyond the *comfort camp* of winning records, acceptable standards, or passing grades. They climb on, always seeking the peak. Which are YOU?

Don't just deal well with adversity but convert it into fuel to achieve greatness. Erik Weihenmayer, in *Adversity Advantage: Turning Everyday Struggles Into Everyday Greatness*

Tuesday - February 12, 2008

Our interim pastor, Dr. Milton Gardner, spoke recently on love. He said that he thinks that he has "**seen love demonstrated more eloquently than I've ever heard anyone explain it.**" He has "seen love on the face of an aged couple sitting…in a nursing home, holding hands and gazing into each other's eyes without a word…a veteran blinded in battle…being told the flag is passing by, rising and snapping a salute…an aged father whose son was arrested, and as he was placed in police custody…cursed his father and the father said 'Son, I love you.'" Love should be said (one source even says that the longest love letter contained "I love you" a total of 1,875,000 times), but it is better when shown. Between coach and player, mentor and student, employer and employee, parent and child, evidence of sincere love, like evidence of an apology, is in action, not in words. If you love somebody or something, tell it, but more importantly, show it.

*For God so **loved** the world, that he **gave** his only begotten Son, that whosoever believeth in him should not perish, but have everlasting life* (emphasis added). John 3:16 KJV

Tuesday - February 19, 2008

Years ago, watching the SEC Softball Championships in Columbus, Georgia with Carie Dever-Boaz, Head Coach at Arkansas, I asked what the biggest problem was coaching at her level. With no hesitation, she said

"Getting players to assume **personal responsibility**." We live in a mixed-up world where fathers carry bat bags, people seek outside answers, educational gurus over-emphasize teacher accountability, and politicians claim that it takes a village to raise a child. I fully believe in the power of teamwork and collective responsibility; but at the core, it is no longer a team game when a hitter enters the batter's box, a shooter steps to the foul line, a student takes a test, or a parent makes a tough decision. To say otherwise or to attempt to mandate anything but personal responsibility is an enormous, critical error. It just will not work. As Winston Churchill said, *"The price of greatness is personal responsibility."* Choose greatness!

You are responsible for everything you think and do, whether you like it, accept it, or even know it.   Jim Newman

Tuesday - February 26, 2008

As I search for neat, little thoughts, I often write the word **myth** next to what I find. Recently, I again saw a saying that sounds good, but is often false. The author said, "If you keep on doing what you've always done, you'll keep on getting what you've always got." It's catchy, but it's a myth. It assumes that you are the only factor in the result. A team or player that keeps doing what they've always done may not keep getting the same result. They may become predictable and an opponent who does the right things better than before may defeat them. A successful business that does what they have always done must often adjust due to market changes. The corporate cemetery is full of those that kept doing what they had always done, but they didn't get what they had always gotten. Successful individuals must do better things or do things better so they can excel. Be careful about accepting thoughts that sound good. Many of them could be myths.

For the Lord gives wisdom; From His mouth come knowledge and understanding; Proverbs 2:6 NKJV

Tuesday - March 4, 2008

So often, I see **people get stuck**. It may be an athlete that reaches a challenge, settles on a plateau, or can't, or just won't, get started when faced with an obstacle. It may be a student who "has no clue" and just does nothing instead of starting to do something to "get a clue." Or, it could be the adult in business, a relationship, or some personal endeavor who faces an uphill battle so he just camps out where he is and refuses to start the climb. Instead of a positive level of *stick-to-it-ness*, they unfortunately have a high level of *stuck-right-here-ness*. When we face the uphill battles of life, whatever the arena, we must refuse to "do nothing." We must get moving, get active, and start doing. Yes, there is often a need for some praying, some planning, and some preparation; but that is doing something. Action must replace the nothing of inertia. Add a big E to motion and get actively energized. Start climbing.

But be doers of the word, and not hearers only, deceiving yourselves.
James 1:22 NKJV

Tuesday - March 11, 2008

I absolutely hate snakes. However, about 10-15 years ago I read an interesting **three-snake rule** used by James Barksdale, the CEO of Netscape, which was an early Internet browser.
Rule #1: *If you see a snake, kill a snake. Don't set up a snake committee. Don't set up a snake user group. Don't write snake memos. Kill it.* He's teaching us that snake time is action time.
Rule #2: *Don't play with dead snakes.* We have a tendency to second-guess our decisions. We should have a solid decision-making procedure, make the best possible decision, and move on. Why revisit and play with a dead snake! Kill it and forget it.
Rule #3: *All opportunities start out looking like snakes.* Improve your snake identification skills. Know a real snake from an artificial snake. Acquire the knowledge, wisdom, and experience that allow you to distinguish truth from myth, real from fake, and genuine from counterfeit.

The people came to Moses and said, "We sinned when we spoke against the Lord and against you. Pray that the Lord will take the snakes away from us." So Moses prayed for the people. Numbers 21:7 NIV

Tuesday - March 18, 2008

While in my early 20's, I did some work helping the Cincinnati Reds with tryout camps. My supervisor, mentor, and friend was a very wise, philosophical scout named George Zuraw. One day while I was coaching at Florida State, he told me that the one item that separated professional players from each other was the **ability to adjust**. As I have coached at numerous levels and in various nations, taught school in two different centuries, led a county recreation department, chaired the youth softball program for the USA's National Governing Body, developed a business, and searched for improvements in family and church, I have found his words to be so applicable. In sports, education, business, relationships, and many other areas, we would do well to give less time to technique, content, or physical skills, and devote much more time to developing skills related to the critical area of effective adjustment. Start now…it's not too late.

It is easier to get mad and make excuses than it is to work hard and make adjustments. Jack Stallings - Former Head Baseball Coach (Wake Forest, Florida State, Georgia Southern)

Tuesday - March 25, 2008

At our church's Easter Sunrise Service, the speaker started by talking about **symbols**, emphasizing the cross and the empty tomb. In my Algebra classes, we discuss the symbol for an operation like addition (+) or a relationship like equality (=). As a third base coach, I would use some body part as a symbol for a bunt or get pleasure when an umpire's spread arms with palms down symbolized a runner being safe. Likewise, the name Cal Ripken is a symbol for class and perseverance in baseball while Lisa Fernandez is a symbol for intense focus and competitiveness in softball. I realized that a symbol is what stands for something or what something stands for. When you consider your team, your group, your business, your family, just what symbol comes to mind? When you truly look inside yourself, what do you stand for? Why not take some time today and see just what you or your group is a symbol of and if the answer is what it should be?

You either stand for something or you'll fall for anything.

Tuesday - April 1, 2008

I am fascinated by how many times I hear a question that asks whether something is one thing **OR** another thing. For example, "Is hitting *linear or rotational*." Then, leaders get asked, "Are you *consistent or flexible* about that." Santa Claus is going to check to see if you are *naughty or nice*. Western movies portray the law wanting the outlaw *dead or alive*. And, the questions go on and on. A week or so ago, I asked my son-in-law if he was going to eat the breakfast that my wife had cooked or eat what would be available a little later at our Sunday School class. His answer was the same as my answer to many of the **OR** questions. He emphatically said **BOTH**! He was not trapped in selecting just one of only two proposed options. Hitting is both. I am *consistently flexible* and *flexibly consistent*. I am usually nice, but have been naughty. I know some people who are alive, but act as if they are dead. Determine today to avoid the **OR TRAP!**

Be lenient where possible and firm where necessary. Bobby Simpson original when in my early 20's

Tuesday - April 8, 2008

I once read a story of an alleged incident when Don Mattingly, a former All-Star for the New York Yankees, was taking pre-game batting practice. Another hitter, waiting his turn in the batter's box, was joking loudly around the cage. Angrily, Mattingly stepped out of the box and told the player to "shut up." He said he was in his office, at work, and resented what the other player was doing. I imagine his words were stronger than that, but you get the point. Mattingly had terrific respect for his workplace, his space. I seek to instill this same **respect for space** in hitters, pitchers, students, and also in anyone else who is working. Respect the batter's box, the pitcher's mound, the fielder's circle, the desk, the cubicle, the classroom, the worksite, the home, or whatever your personal space may be. Use it as a place for improvement and excellence. Treat it as "holy ground." Constantly ask yourself, "Is where I am a better place because *I* am there?"

"Do not come any closer," God said. "Take off your sandals, for the place where you are standing is holy ground." Exodus 3:5 NIV

Tuesday - April 15, 2008

Last year, I viewed a Power Point presentation from a Canadian forum related to achieving goals. One speaker made a very astute observation about **teamwork** and I wish to share it word for word. Keep it in mind as you journey in today's over-emphasis on cloning in athletic mechanics, corporate benchmarking, societal values, educational achievement, fashion, style, and many more areas of our lives. A singular principle or goal often involves many methods.

*Together gears perform tasks at a rate that makes machines run quicker, smoother, and more efficient. As a team of **gears works in unison** behind the scenes they are **moving in different directions and at different speeds**; linked together they each have their own responsibility, but the same goal. You are an integral part of our team, allowing us to work better together and in turn driving us to success* (emphasis added).
Ainsley B. Rose

Tuesday - April 22, 2008

I love catchy phrases. One that is frequently used to describe proper preparation is "Ready, willing, and able." While that is often a nice condition, the fact is that we must often perform when the condition is not so nice. We must achieve success when we are "**Unready, unable, and**

willing." Far too often, a hitter gets fooled by a 2-strike pitch, concedes defeat, holds the bat, and loses the pitcher-hitter battle. But, the great hitter can get fooled, decide to fight, and be willing to win the battle with the 40 percent she has left. Daily, I see students say they have no clue, write *dnk* (do not know), leave a question blank, and lose the test-student battle. Sadly, the story is frequently repeated in the work place and the arena of personal relationships. If you are unready and unable, be willing. Swing the bat, pick up the pencil, grab the tools, start the process, endure the struggle. With a willing start, you often gain readiness and become able.

The greatest composer does not sit down to work because he is inspired, but becomes inspired because he is working. Ernest Newman – English music critic (1868-1959)

Tuesday - April 29, 2008

Today, I'd like for you to consider some more **inequalities**, where things do not equal what many think they do. Some are quotes and some are my thoughts. I trust you will find them helpful.

Doing more does not equal doing better…Looking does not equal seeing…Seeing does not equal understanding…Happiness does not equal joy…Listening does not equal hearing…Hearing does not equal understanding…Balance does not equal control…1+1 does not always equal 2…You plus Me does not always equal Us…Conceiving and believing does not equal achieving…A reason that sounds good does not equal a good sound reason…Hard work does not equal good effort…Potential does not equal performance…Treating people equally does not equal treating people fairly…Certified does not equal qualified.

For then there will be great distress, unequaled from the beginning of the world until now—and never to be equaled again. Matthew 24:21 NIV

Tuesday - May 6, 2008

Recently, I received a newsletter from a good friend of mine. He wrote that many websites contain misspelled words. He recommended that at least four pair of eyes look over items before release. Prior to her death in 1978, my mother was the proofreader for the local newspaper. Recently, one of her former colleagues told me that there were a lot fewer mistakes when she was there in the days before computers than there are today with all the sophisticated spell check programs. I agree. She was a terrific recognizer and caring fixer. I got to thinking that this is what helps to make mothers so special. Just as my mother fixed broken communication in the paper and breaks in my life, many fix things like a doll's arm, a tricycle wheel, a broken table leg, or a teenager's heart. Use your very best thoughts, words, and actions to give much deserved thanks to your mother or the mother of your children. Determine to **be a fixer**.

Your people will rebuild the ancient ruins and will raise up the age-old foundations; you will be called Repairer of Broken Walls, Restorer of Streets with Dwellings. Isaiah 58:12 NIV

Tuesday - May 13, 2008

I love to see a young person mess up. That seems to be an odd statement from someone who spends so much time seeking to help young athletes and students improve. Actually, I love to see how they recover (overcome or minimize damage) when they mess up singing, make an error, give up a home run, miss lines in a drama, strike out, or make much lower on a test than normal. In recent weeks, I have seen a student who normally makes strong A's make a low C on a test. That student rebounded with three straight grades of 100 or higher. I saw a young person miss the words and notes early in a solo, but rebound to finish strong. And, during a hitting lesson with a player who'll play college softball in about a year, I saw terrific **bounceability** as she battled back from failing the very difficult challenge I gave her for about 45 minutes. I measure the critical **bounceability** factor by recovery quickness and height. They measured well. You?

If you are made of the right stuff, a hard fall results in a high bounce.
Coach Bacevich and others

Tuesday - May 20, 2008

I confess. A few months ago, attending a full-day seminar for several hundred people, I spent much time reading a very good book, *The Age Of Speed*, written by Vince Poscente, an Olympic speed skier. He discussed whether multitasking speeds us up or slows us down. He said we once lived in a linear world, but we now live in a much different world, starting, shifting, and finishing multiple tasks within a time frame. This happens in school, athletics, and on the job. To be more effective, singular focus on one task may not be enough. We must be able to **toggle** from one action to another and then back again. "We must balance the speed benefits that interruptions and multitasking can provide with the clear drag they exert." A proper arousal level is needed to improve performance so "we must allow disruptions that add speed, but avoid the ones that detract from it." I feel better. I think he would agree with my *book-to-speaker toggles*.

We have to take control over what interruptions we accept and when we choose to accept them – when to multitask and when to focus. Vince Poscente

Tuesday - May 27, 2008

A few months ago, I saw a terrific thought posted in a school leader's office. It stated that "Our role is not to prepare the path for the student, rather **prepare the student** for the path." This powerful message is critical in athletics, education, the family, and the corporate world. We must help people develop qualities like responsibility, integrity, work ethic, trust, commitment, compassion, enthusiasm, courage, and the ability to adjust. Far too often, coaches, educators, parents, and corporate leaders are trying to prepare a magic path, when we should be developing a solid person who can assist in creating the path, improving the path, and adjusting to the potholes in the path. Instead of cloning mechanics, we should develop the person so he can find a path that works for him. Let's begin to focus on the person, so the person can improve his ability to recognize the proper path and adjust so that he can properly travel that route to success.

Our role is not to prepare the path for the student, rather prepare the student for the path. Ainsley B. Rose (It is so important that I said it twice on purpose – Bobby)

Tuesday - June 3, 2008

A few days ago, I had a very enjoyable email exchange with Linda Wells (former Head Coach of Arizona State and the 2004 Greek Olympic Team, and currently an assistant with the 2008 Dutch Olympic Team). Then, this past Sunday we opened our church service singing "This Is The Day." Combining Linda, the Dutch, and the song made me recall August, 1999, when I was in Holland helping Craig Montvidas work with a fine group of young ladies on one of their Junior National Teams. Watching TV, I heard a Dutch choir sing "Dit Is De Dag (This Is The Day)." I also recalled Rico Schuijers, the fine Dutch sports psychologist, encouraging players and coaches to ask **WDWDN**…What Do We Do NOW? Whether it is an upcoming pitch, the reflection on a completed game, an important life decision, a coaching move, or an issue at work or in a relationship, NOW is a critical time. This IS the day. Be glad. Wise action is possible NOW!

This is the day which the LORD hath made; we will rejoice and be glad in it. Psalm 118:24 KJV

Tuesday - June 10, 2008

Looking through a file of old items that I clipped years ago, I ran across some wisdom from the late Boston Red Sox slugger Ted Williams, the last Major League hitter to bat over .400 for a season. It seems that he "once advised a not-so-bright teammate, 'If you don't think too good, then **don't think too much**.'" My wife would call that common sense, but then I've told her that in today's world "common sense is not too common."

Anyway, Williams' advice is something that all too often goes unheeded. Too many hitters swing at pitches they don't normally hit well and pitchers end up looking a lot better than they really are. Too many businesses attempt to do something they aren't very good at and get poor results. Too many people say or write too many words about things they really don't know much about and look foolish. Yes, too many of us suffer from "paralysis by analysis" and lose rhythm, timing, and effectiveness. Thanks, Ted.

And when you pray, do not keep on babbling like pagans, for they think they will be heard because of their many words. Matthew 6:7 NIV

Tuesday - June 17, 2008

Years ago, I heard a story about some animals that were living on the farm of an orphanage. It seems that the people who lived or worked at the orphanage had been very kind to the animals so the animals decided to do something nice for them. They discussed a lot of ideas, but could not come up with something that they thought would adequately show their sincere appreciation to the people at the orphanage. Finally, excited with her own idea, one of the hens flapped her wings wildly and leaped up to say, "They all love to eat, so why don't we give them a huge ham and egg breakfast!" That seemed like a good idea until a hog rose to say, "That may be fine for you hens since you are only making a contribution, but it's quite different for us hogs…we are being asked to make a commitment." What about you? In your team, your job, or your relationship, **are you a hen or a hog**?

Now, to show my commitment to the temple of my God, I donate my personal treasure of gold and silver to the temple of my God, in addition to all that I have already supplied for this holy temple. 1 Chronicles 29: 3 NET

Tuesday - June 24, 2008

I am still on Cloud 9, pumped, excited. Our Higher Ground SUPER & SELECT Softball Camp For Advanced and Elite Skills ended last Friday, but I am still energized by the enthusiasm of the young ladies who attended. In the best-seller *If It Ain't Broke...BREAK IT*, Robert J. Kriegel says, "I interviewed over 500 top performers from all areas of work, the arts, and sports. No two were alike, but the one quality they had in common was *passion!* It was their drive, their enthusiasm, and their desire that distinguished them. They were passionate and excited about what they were doing." I see the same **passion, drive, and enthusiasm** each year at this camp and I come away a year younger for having spent time absorbing that enthusiasm. At times, I may see apathy in today's youth, but then I get blessed to spend a week each summer charging up my energy cell. These special young ladies are *energy adders*, not *energy leaks*. What about you?

*Incredibly as it may sound; yes, they can get up in the morning; yes, they will listen; yes, they are just teenagers; and, finally, yes, every one of them are thrilled...*From email sent by a player's father who observed the 2007 camp, sent as he stopped in Jordan on way to Iraq.

Tuesday - July 1, 2008

A young lady who was always happy when she came for hitting lessons arrived really down on one particular night. She had hit poorly in recent games and was discouraged, confused by conflicting advice, and extremely frustrated. After a very open discussion about the situation and possible causes, we went to work. The brakes of poor confidence, high frustration, and confusion slowed her explosive swing and she looked bad. After 15 minutes, I told her to just install her *good goofiness*. She was a fun-loving, yet serious, player and acting *goofy* at times was very relaxing for her. After bad swings, she turned her back to the plate, began to *walk away like an Egyptian*, loudly stating, "Just walk away." Soon, having fun and relaxing, she began to whip the bat and hit shot after shot. At times, **we may need to walk away for a moment,** so we become more effective in a game, a job, or a relationship. *Good goofiness* may be critical to a good job.

And after he had dismissed the crowds, he went up on the mountain by himself to pray. When evening came, he was there alone, Matthew 14:23 ESV

Tuesday - July 8, 2008

I do not play golf. It takes too long, the holes seem longer than the card says, and hustle does not help me win. However, I read golf books, especially those about the mental approach. I'm reading *Mind Over Golf*, written in 1993 by Dr. Richard Coop, and he reminded me of the value of **proper self-talk**. Not unique to golf or sport, it can be used with any skill…typing, carpentry, public speaking…The key is to get it to help you increase the odds of doing better. You talk to yourself a lot, so be nice. I take 5 minutes and $5.00 to get a haircut, look in the mirror, and say that I look fine. Some people take 100 minutes and $100, look in the mirror, and criticize how they look. Replace the personal *bad-mouth* with self-encouragement. We encourage our friends when they mess up, but we beat up on ourselves. Coop suggests that we imagine our mistakes as someone else's and then encourage them. I like that idea. Try it today when you mess up. Be nice to you.

Decide in advance what you're going to say to yourself…You'll be a bit like an actor who has learned lines in preparation for a stage performance. Dr. Richard Coop

Tuesday - July 15, 2008

I was looking at some options for today's thought and ran across an email that my daughter, Neilie, sent me almost five years ago. It was a collection of six of her favorite thoughts, **more or less** a summary of some key principles that mean a lot to her. They were all very helpful and I needed the reminder that was contained in each message. However, as I read them this morning, one just seemed to pop out as very timely and insightful. So,

I am just going to quit writing and copy that quote below. I **wish** YOU a more joy filled day as you apply these words a daughter shared with her father.

Don't wish it was easier; wish you were better. Don't wish for less problems; wish for more skills. Don't wish for less challenges; wish for more wisdom. Jim Rohn

Tuesday - July 22, 2008

If you talk to Bonnie, my wife, or Christie, my office manager, they will tell you that one of my weaknesses is that I do not always listen as well as I should. I say that they just forget to tell me the things that they say I did not hear, but you know who wins that argument (Hint: not Bobby). Anyway, I do need to improve my **listening skills**. On the other side of the coin, be careful just who you do listen to. In Pat Williams' book, *Go For The Magic*, he quotes playwright Neil Simon, who said, "Don't listen to those who say, 'It's not done that way!' Maybe it's not, but maybe you'll do it anyway. Don't listen to those who say, 'You're taking too big a chance.' Michelangelo would have painted the Sistine floor, and it would surely be rubbed out today." Pay close attention to those players, employees, or others who don't seem to listen. Just maybe some of them will be the Michelangelo that finds another way to paint success in your arena.

Listen to counsel and receive instruction, That you may be wise in your latter days. Proverbs 19:20 NKJV

Tuesday - July 29, 2008

In 1999, Craig Montvidas invited me to Holland to assist the Dutch National Team in a series of games with the Australian National Team. They were preparing for an Olympic Qualifier that could gain them a berth in the 2000 Sydney Olympics. He knew that the Australians were stronger, so he wisely scheduled 4-inning double-headers instead of 7-inning games. On the first day, Dutch captain Erica Bol, facing very tough pitching, struck out her first 4-5 at-bats. I knew Erica as a competitor, so I was extremely proud of her reaction to the strikeouts. After the last one, she went to the end of the bench, immediately encouraging the next hitter, yelling "Come on, you can do it." Her ability to **externalize** and improve her future performance showed strong mental skills and superb teamwork. In your difficulties, will you put on *pooch lips* and pout at the self-pity party, or follow the example of a fine Dutch player and properly externalize?

Therefore encourage one another and build each other up, just as in fact you are doing. 1 Thessalonians 5:11 NIV

Tuesday - August 5, 2008

A few weeks ago, our Associate Pastor began a series of sermons on Jesus' use of the phrase "I am…," (*the way, the bread of life,* etc.) and I positively know Jesus spoke truthfully. I have considered those two words for several years and I get a little upset with people who do something a certain way, especially if I do not like their attitude, and then say, "That's just **the way I am**." I tell coaches, players, and whoever else will listen, "You can change *the way you am*." I know that may be improper use of the English language, but it is understood. So, it is an effective means of communication. We should not use *the way we am* as an excuse for lack of commitment, poor work ethic, ineffective performance, or misdirected leadership. If needed, change *the way you am*. Oh, before I forget, Bonnie and I are going to be grandparents. Neilie and Justin are expecting their first child (our first grandchild) in late February. We am blessed!

Jesus said to him, "I am the way, the truth, and the life. No one comes to the Father except through Me. John 14:6 NKJV

Tuesday - August 12, 2008

I recently recalled "Turn, Turn, Turn," a popular song that I liked when I was younger. Written in the 1950's by Pete Seeger, the version I enjoyed was released in 1965 by a folk-rock band called the Byrds, and featured in the 1994 movie *Forrest Gump*. The words are almost exactly those found in the King James Version of the Bible in Ecclesiastes 3:1-8. The central message is that there is a time and place (a season) for almost all things. We must be careful about the timing of our actions. I may be right if I tell my wife something, but I'm in a heap of trouble if I tell her at the wrong time. My message may be positively correct when I say it to a player, but it can be just as positively the wrong time to say it and the result can be disastrous. If the message is good and the timing is bad, the odds of a good result are small. So, before your actions, take time to make sure it's **the right time**.

To every thing there is a season, and a time to every purpose under the heaven: Ecclesiastes 3:1 KJV

Tuesday - August 19, 2008

When I was 25, I spent the summer working for the Kansas City Royals Baseball Academy, conducting tryout camps and serving as an instructor/coach for their team in the Gulf Coast Rookie League. On my very first day in Sarasota, Buzzy Keller, the manager, inserted me as the first base coach. A few weeks later, when he went to Kansas City for some organizational meetings, he named me acting manager for three days. So what? Well, he had three veteran coaches on his staff including a pitching coach who had been in the Major Leagues for many years, a former winner of the American League batting title, and Joe Tanner, a guy who created many innovative techniques and a batting tee still used today by almost all MLB teams. The **So What** is that he made the *new guy on the block* feel welcome and **instilled confidence** in me. How well do we follow Buzzy's very wise concept of leadership through a *trusting action*?

And the natives showed us unusual kindness; for they kindled a fire and made us all welcome, because of the rain that was falling and because of the cold. Acts 28:2 NKJV

Tuesday - August 26, 2008

It may surprise you, but one of my favorite movies is *Notting Hill*. Filmed in 1999, it was ranked in 2004 as one of the top 50 *chick flicks* of all-time. Julia Roberts plays Anna Scott, a megastar American actress who, while filming in London, has an on-and-off romance with an everyday local bookstore owner, William Thacker, played by Hugh Grant. You can imagine the obstacles of such a relationship, with one so famous and the other a regular person. After several attempts to make it work, Anna comes to the bookstore and asks William to try one more time. He says NO, citing that she is famous and he is just a regular person. Her next line is a nugget for all of us, "Right now, I'm just a girl, standing in front of a boy, asking him to love her." How marvelously she condensed the complex to the simple. That's also our job as we communicate. Take the complex and **make it simple**. Right now, let's all determine to do a better job at that.

Since hitting is difficult, we should make our explanation simple. Jack Stallings - retired as third-winningest NCAA college baseball coach (Wake Forest, Florida State, Georgia Southern)

Tuesday - September 2, 2008

Long ago, I realized that you only need a pretty good swing to be a very good hitter. You also can have a very good swing and not be a good hitter at all. Athletes can spend too much time on the physical component and not enough on the mental component. Too often, I see brakes put on the physical by the evil forces of fear, frustration, tension, low confidence, or other such sinister gremlins. Therefore, much of my instruction involves a joint effort by the athlete and myself to unleash the skills that are already there, to **release the brakes** and let loose the wonderful forces already inside the person whom I am helping. In 1999, while on a trip with me to speak at the Italian National Clinic, my wife, daughter, and I visited Florence and viewed Michelangelo's famous statue of *David*. About a month later, I read Daryl Conner's book, *Managing at the Speed of*

Change, and his words below reminded me to help others **Unleash the Power**.

Michelangelo once claimed that he did not really create the figures he carved in marble. They were already in the stone; he simply chipped away the excess so that they could be seen. Daryl Conner

Tuesday - September 9, 2008

A few weeks ago, Donny Amrein did a team clinic for us at Randolph Southern, a private school in Shellman, Georgia. When I met him and the coach to get our equipment at the end of the last day, one player still remained waiting for her parents to pick her up. Donny was kidding her about being someone who would *stir things up* at practice. I have always felt that successful teams and organizations need someone who is willing to *stir things up*, to question the status quo, to follow Bob Kriegel's book title of *If It Ain't Broke…BREAK IT*. Too often, people fear the consequences of disagreement. They fear conflict, not realizing that conflict is not always destructive. It can also be productive. Coaches, parents, and other leaders must sometimes have the wisdom and courage to bring conflict to the surface so that the group can productively journey through the struggles of a storm. Stirring the pot just might produce a better flavor.

…teams that trust one another…do not hesitate to disagree with, challenge, and question one another, all in the spirit of finding the best answers, discovering the truth, and making great decisions. Patrick Lencioni, in *Overcoming The Five Dysfunctions Of A Team*

Tuesday - September 16, 2008

Sometimes I start to type, but I am not quite sure where I'll end up. Keep reading…let's see. On a walk from my house to my office, I saw a political notice hung on my door by a **rubber band**. I was carrying several items and at that very moment, I needed just that size rubber band to hold everything together. It was a little thing, but it was very important.

It met my need. Do we often neglect the little things that players, coaches, or others might need right at that moment so they can hold everything together? Maybe the pitcher needs to know it's okay that she gave up the hit…maybe the hitter needs to know it's okay that she struck out. Maybe it's not the advice on pitching or health care, but rather the right word, the smile, the arm around the shoulder, the pat on the back. I was gonna vote for that man anyway, but now every rubber band I see will remind me to help others **hold it all together**. Thanks for staying with me…I kinda like where it ended.

Enjoy the little things, for one day you may look back and realize they were the big things. Robert Brault

Tuesday - September 23, 2008

Cyndi Thomson, a young lady from my hometown, had the number one song on the country music charts. It was entitled "What I Really Meant To Say," and on the CD there was another song entitled "If You Could Only See." Pardon me, but I'd like to change that last title to "What We're Really Meant To See." I often hear people who love video analysis say that pictures don't lie. Oh, but they do! The interpretation of the viewer, the angle of viewing, or emphasis placed on some parts of the picture can easily present a misleading analysis. Cyndi's song said that she wished the boy could see in himself what she saw in him. We wish the same for people that we know. We all need to work at a more accurate view of others and ourselves. My friend Vicky Rogers says that she never sees a coin on the ground…rather she sees a reminder in the words *In God We Trust* that are inscribed. Let's all improve our skill at seeing **What We're Really Meant To See**.

For since the creation of the world God's invisible qualities—his eternal power and divine nature—have been clearly seen, being understood from what has been made, so that people are without excuse. Romans 1:20 NIV

Tuesday - September 30, 2008

In 1993-1996, I conducted clinics in Wilmington, NC for Payton Warren and Tom Crawford. Tom, a General Electric executive, recently sent a message about **The Butterfly Principle**. Part of it read, "The caterpillar that lies inside the cocoon will never become the beautiful butterfly if someone cuts open the cocoon prematurely. It is **the struggle** that allows the butterfly to emerge as a strong, new creature of nature." A few days later, I read that a school had listed its mission as "Failure is not an option." In a misguided effort to help others, too many fall for that fallacy. They want to liberalize life and guarantee success. Seeking to eliminate the struggle or failure, they remove the personal responsibility that is vital. PLEASE allow failure…cherish the value of the struggle at the field, job, classroom, and home. Quit being so overprotective, wrap your arms lovingly around the cocoons, and allow your caterpillars to become truly beautiful butterflies.

Develop success from failures. Discouragement and failure are two of the surest stepping stones to success. Dale Carnegie

Success is going from failure to failure without losing your enthusiasm. Abraham Lincoln

Tuesday - October 7, 2008

One of my all-time favorite books, *Hope Is Not A Method*, written by former Army Chief of Staff Gordon R. Sullivan and Michael V. Harper, discusses an effort to "take the best army in the world and make it the best army in a different world." Our role must be very similar as we seek to take what we have now and make it the best in **something that comes later**. Whether working to help ourselves or help others, we should seek to make something better for the future. Since the future will likely be different than the present, we should most often have a goal of preparing for the future rather than measuring immediate success. Our athletic practice must not be judged by how good it appears, but by how well it prepares us for the future game. The parent must prepare the child for a future that is different than the present. The educator must not be satisfied with graduation rate, but rather emphasize proper preparation for success in a future world.

Today's problems can be so close, so intense, that they become like blinders. Getting beyond today begins by imagining…out in the future. Sullivan & Harper

Tuesday - October 14, 2008

In *Better Than Good*, Zig Ziglar tells us that the Second Law of Thermodynamics says that, in a closed system, disorder increases and energy decreases. That also seems to apply to people. I see athletes, workers, students, or other associates who run out of energy, enthusiasm, or passion. I also am thankful when people compliment me for having a lot of energy and passion. **Without help, energy decreases**, so I tell myself to inject inspiration by reading, writing, speaking, moving quicker, becoming active, or laughing. Gloria Beard, a teaching friend, says she took more notes if she got tired or bored when she was a student. Davy Jones, lead singer of the popular 1960's group the *Monkees*, told me he jumped up and down and ran all over the stage whenever he did not want to perform, and was energized in less than a minute. Lack of energy can normally be corrected with frequent rekindling and inspiration. Get active…get energy.

Passion will die without constant injections of new inspiration…it's a lifelong responsibility for us to stir up and rekindle the gifts God has given us. Zig Ziglar

Tuesday - October 21, 2008

I once read a very interesting item about Roman construction. I knew that one of the features of Roman architecture was the use of arches. I also knew that many of the structures that are over 2000 years old are still standing. What I did not know, until I read that item about fifteen years ago, was why their structures may still be standing. It seems that when the arches of a structure were finished, the engineer in charge was required to stand under the arches until the scaffolding was removed. If it was not built well, he would be the very first one to know and it could be a very painful lesson that would be learned. Talk about emphasizing **personal responsibility**! Ask yourself if you are willing to stand under your constructions. Are you willing to stand under the teams, businesses, families, friendships, or projects that you have built? Let ***some roads lead from Rome*** and stand under the arches of lives that you help to construct with excellence.

Whatever you do, work at it with all your heart, as working for the Lord, not for human masters, Colossians 3:23 NIV

Tuesday - October 28, 2008

Early on the morning of February 9, 2008, I went outside to get in my van and go to the office. I heard a lot of noise from Mrs. Kincaid's screen porch next door and noticed that a large bird had somehow flown into the enclosed porch but could not get out. In an effort to be helpful, I tried to hold the door open while attempting to use a broom to entice the bird to leave. Unsuccessful, I then went to wake up my *non-morning-person* wife and asked her to hold the door open while I beat on the screen with the broom to get the bird out. She suggested that I prop the door open with the broom and beat on the screen with my hands. Wow!! This guy, me, who teaches people in sports and other areas of life to make better use of their resources, had just had a half-awake person teach him how to use a resource better. It's a simple story with a solid lesson: let's resolve to seek a greater awareness of **resources** and become more effective in our use of them.

A wise man *will hear and increase learning, And a man of understanding will attain wise counsel,* Proverbs 1:5 NKJV

Tuesday - November 4, 2008

In a recent article in *NFCA Fastpitch Delivery*, Carie Dever-Boaz, one of the finest pitching instructors and ladies in softball, stated that many pitchers claim to throw six or more pitches, but have mastered few, if any, of them. On Sunday, Milton Gardner's sermon mentioned that someone said that America's spirituality is wide but very thin. As an educator, I fear that today's philosophy is cloning too many students to be broad, but often shallow. As a coach, I understand the value of the utility player. As a homeowner with few homeowner skills, I highly value the handyman. However, I also am convinced that a team of too many utility players would have trouble winning and a construction company too heavy on handymen would soon go out of business. *Wide and thin* is definitely a "clear and present danger," so let's examine our personal situation and see if **deep and wide** or maybe even **deep and narrow** are better options.

that Christ may dwell in your hearts through faith; that you, being rooted and grounded in love, may be able to comprehend with all the saints what is the width and length and depth and height — to know the love of Christ which passes knowledge; that you may be filled with all the fullness of God. Ephesians 3:17-19 NKJV

Tuesday - November 11, 2008

Rosie Leutzinger, University of Washington All-American, played on the British National Team that I coached and had as good a softball **awareness and expectancy** as I've ever seen. In an Olympic Qualifier game, she hit a one-hopper to the pitcher and our runner on second was trapped in a rundown as she mistakenly took off for third. If unable to escape, a runner is taught to delay the out so that the trail runner can get to second, with the hitter taught to think two bases. Rosie expected three bases! Refusing to be upset about the bouncer to the pitcher, she raced to second. As the third baseman tagged our runner, Rosie edged toward third. The fielder walked toward the mound, tossing the ball to the pitcher. Rosie sprinted to third, sliding to the back corner and avoiding the tag on a rushed throw from a surprised pitcher. Some think two, but a prepared Rosie got three. Do you settle for two when better expectancy allows you to get three?

And they exceeded our expectations: They gave themselves first of all to the Lord, and then by the will of God also to us. 2 Corinthians 8:5 NIV

Tuesday - November 18, 2008

I have often heard someone say, "Anything worth doing is worth doing well." It's a nice thought and sometimes it is correct, but it is also often incorrect or incomplete. A number of years ago, while serving as Chairman of the ASA National Junior Olympic Softball Committee, I was involved in a project with Dr. Peter Pierro, an educational psychologist from Oklahoma City. He altered the thought above to state, "Anything worth doing is worth doing poorly…at first." As I thought about it, I agreed. What if the baby's first step had to be done well, the hitter had to make a mental or physical adjustment immediately, a musician had to be able to play a song correctly the first time, or a parent had to do the job well from day one? We already have enough people who want instant gratification or *microwaved success*. It is vital that we realize that many of the *anythings* take time and that we must often **be willing to look bad to become good.**

Peak performance is dependent on passion, grit, determination, and a willingness to do something poorly until you can do it well. Zig Ziglar

Tuesday - November 25, 2008

On Saturday, my wife and I went to Savannah, Georgia for the wedding of Mandy Morelock and Clint Whitley. My daughter Neilie, six-months pregnant, was a bridesmaid. The next day, we drove back to Tifton, changed very quickly, and drove 75 miles to Americus for the funeral of Edra Pope, grandmother of my daughter's lifelong friend. As I drove part of the 600 miles, I realized how the **past, present, and future** were represented…Mrs. Pope, as we grieved but celebrated her wonderful past, the deep joy of the present moment during vows spoken by Mandy and Clint, and the visualized magic for my future grandson, Cullen, who began life six months ago and will be officially welcomed to Earth in February.

Some advise us to focus on the present moment. Actually, we should be thankful for the past, present, and future. Use your past experiences to increase confidence…imagine success in the future…together, that increases odds for joy in the present.

"I am the Alpha and the Omega, the Beginning and the End," says the Lord, "who is and who was and who is to come, the Almighty." Revelations 1:8 NKJV

Tuesday - December 2, 2008

Syd Thrift passed away about two months ago. He served in many capacities in professional baseball and was the General Manager for several MLB teams. As Director of the KC Royals Baseball Academy, he hired me in 1972 to run tryouts and coach in the Gulf Coast Rookie League. His favorite question was "**WHY**," and the academy led to many innovations (elastic bands, silver-gray underside on cap bills, video taping, sports vision, use of color to affect anxiety levels, fielding techniques, etc.) as he challenged tradition. *Why* don't we ask **WHY** when we know that players are unique, but hitting instructors want to clone them all to use the same technique; when students have different experiences and future needs but we propose the same curriculum, standard tests, and graduation requirements; when situations are different, but we want the same rules in a policy manual? *Why* don't we have the courage to ask **WHY**?

"Ask, and it will be given to you; seek, and you will find; knock, and it will be opened to you." Matthew 7:7 NKJV

Tuesday - December 9, 2008

I fully believe in the value of **good questions**, since they help you collect information that is complete, accurate, appropriate, and useful. I strongly recommend that you carefully consider **who to ask**. A leading cultural institution was about to pay a large sum to a consultant to find out which exhibit was the most popular. Then, a wise member of the committee suggested that they simply ask the janitor where he had to mop the most.

Ask the students walking on campus where sidewalks need to be or simply check the worn grass. In their youth, asking how to improve at little expense, Pete Rose hit a ball hung from a rope and Harmon Killebrew hit flower bushes. They became two of the best hitters ever. Remember to ask *non-gurus*. A LOT of times, my wife, with limited softball knowledge, has given me, a self-appointed guru, extremely wise solutions that I did not see. Ask yourself and others how to ask better questions and how to better ask questions.

Plans fail for lack of counsel, but with many advisers they succeed.
Proverbs 15:22 NIV

Tuesday - December 16, 2008

Last spring, while I was attending a softball tournament, a father asked me to watch his daughter in her next game. I actually do not get to sit and watch games very often, but I decided I'd watch the teenage shortstop. They hit her a little spinning popup between short and third and she easily got there, but dropped it. What she did next really impressed me. Instead of staging a *pity party* and walking to get the ball, she scrambled after it and **quickly** checked every runner on base to see if she could get anyone out at another base. That is what she should do…**recover and minimize the damage**…but far too few do that. At a very young age, she knew the importance of a recovery plan. Whether your mistakes involve actions at the softball field, the corporate office, the classroom, or the home, or are as simple as failing to follow your diet, make sure that you plan ahead and develop the principles of a recovery plan. It's a vital ingredient for success.

People make mistakes, and yet some find a way to **quickly** *get back on track rather than sink further in despair* (emphasis added). Simple, yet powerful principle from the excellent book, *Influencer: The Power To Change Anything,* by Kerry Patterson, Joseph Grenny, David Maxfield, Ron McMillan, and Al Switzler.

Tuesday - December 23, 2008

Last week, my wife kept reminding me to take the card and gift on the kitchen table and give them to a lady at school. On Friday, I took the gift. On Saturday, my wife asked me why I did not take the card, which contained the gift certificate that was the main gift. I could not come up with a very good answer. Neither of us touched the thermostat, but the atmosphere in the house suddenly got colder. Odd how a man can get in hot water, but the temperature goes down! This reminds me of the Christmas song entitled, "Do You Hear What I Hear?" Bonnie clearly said it more than once, but I did not hear it because my mind was somewhere else. At this time of year, let's **determine to hear better** the message that is being spoken. Whether it's the coach and player talking, the employer – employee conversation, the discussion with a friend or family member, or God telling us the true meaning of CHRISTmas, may we get our mind where it needs to be and hear better.

My sheep hear My voice, and I know them, and they follow Me. John 10:27 NKJV

Tuesday - December 30, 2008

In July, 2003, after pouring our hearts into nearly 20 months of underdog preparation, the British National Team that I coached was eliminated late in the ISF Olympic Qualifier Tournament. As we gathered in leftfield, I told the team that I didn't know what to say, since I had not planned on losing. That night, I slept very little in the hotel in Macerata, Italy, but the next morning I had a message...**we hurt, we learn, we move on**. On August 21, 2007, our beloved pastor of ten years followed God's call to another church. Speaking the next night at our Wednesday prayer service, I had the same core message…we hurt, we learn, we move on. Two days ago, our new pastor preached a sermon entitled, *Forward In Faith*, suggesting that we get over the past, avoid being enamored by the present, and move forward in faith. Whatever you encountered this past year, I encourage you to learn from it, even if you were hurt, and move on with faith and confidence.

Pressing on the upward way, new heights I'm gaining every day; still praying as I onward bound, Lord, plant my feet on higher ground. From hymn, "Higher Ground," by Johnson Oatman, Jr., 1898

THOUGHTS FOR TUESDAY
GOLD MEDAL WISDOM FOR LIFE

2009

*The way of a fool is right in his own eyes, But he who heeds counsel is **wise** (emphasis added). Proverbs 12:15 NKJV*

Tuesday - January 6, 2009

I bought it about five years ago, but I did not read Mary Lou Retton's *Gateways to Happiness* until about two weeks ago. Shortly after the 1984 Olympics, when a reporter asked how she had done all that she did (injuries, pain, etc.) to win the Gold, the former Olympic gymnast gave a fantastic answer. She said, "You know, I think it's really about heart. Every great achievement is the story of a **flaming heart**...tremendous passion." She gave that answer at age 17. At age 32, she wrote, "Children possess a remarkable amount of passion. They throw themselves completely, heart and soul, into everything, whether it's building a house out of wooden blocks, or trying to get away with not eating their green beans…sadly, most of us never try to follow our passion…the mundane world of the practical takes over…" Let us all turn off the automatic pilot, reacquire childlike energy, and move forward with a **flaming heart**.

Being passionate means…allowing yourself to feel deeply about whatever issues are at stake and to become personally invested in the outcome of a project or circumstance. Mary Lou Retton

Tuesday - January 13, 2009

You may have seen the Internet version of *The Last Lecture* by Randy Pausch, who at the time of his last lecture was a terminally ill computer science professor at Carnegie Mellon. If you haven't seen it, promise yourself that you will. He also wrote a short, extremely enlightening book by the same title and fortunately I received it as a Christmas present (twice). In one chapter, he discussed a visit that William Shatner (Captain Kirk, commander of the *Starship Enterprise* on the hit TV show, *Star Trek*), made to his virtual lab at Carnegie Mellon. He described Shatner as "a man who **knew what he didn't know**, was perfectly willing to admit it, and didn't want to leave until he understood." What a combination of qualities…to be so aware, to know thyself, be perfectly willing to admit what you don't know, and to hunger with stamina for understanding.

Coaches, players, business executives…ah, all of us…should seek to board that *Enterprise*.

Shatner stayed for three hours and asked tons of questions…I was hugely impressed. Randy Pausch

Tuesday - January 20, 2009

Recently, I spoke at the Georgia Dugout Club Clinic in Atlanta. Wonderful people and clinic, plus fantastic item in my room at the Hilton. Each end table beside my bed had a motion detector in it. At night, when I got up, a small beam of light guided me…the same happened when I returned. At home, my wife likes to sleep in the darkest dark and I like light. So, the compromise is a sister-in-law gift of a night-light that gives a slight glow in the room, just enough so I don't walk into a wall. The Hilton has the answer…dark until light is needed, and then enough light to do the job without blinding anyone. As we coach athletes, teach students, train employees, or raise children, we need that principle. Provide enough enlightenment to help them, but don't do it all. Give a glow, but let them have enough personal responsibility to discover the brightest and best ways. Reject over-structured cloning. Allow imagination so they learn to **light the way.**

There are two kinds of light - the glow that illumines, and the glare that obscures. James Thurber

Tuesday - January 27, 2009

Crossing the line usually implies going too far in a behavior. Let's see if we can reframe it as a positive action. Teach hitters to properly cross the line of the batter's box, leaving thinking on the outside and taking trust to the inside. Show young ladies how to leave other roles outside as they cross the line of the gate to the field, becoming a softball player. When I coached at FSU, you had to become a Seminole baseball player when you crossed the short wooden bridge that led to the field. Tony Muser, former MLB manager, used the foul line as a *work line* and players could not talk with opponents on the fair side. Perhaps a doorway will allow you to transform to a student or employee as you cross the line into a classroom or office. Better yet, maybe you can hang the work issues on the *worry tree* outside the front door as you cross the line from work to home. Let's all improve our skills at **crossing the line**.

Do not conform to the pattern of this world, but be transformed by the renewing of your mind. Then you will be able to test and approve what God's will is—his good, pleasing and perfect will. Romans 12: 2 NIV

Tuesday - February 3, 2009

Charles Dieas, a good church friend of mine, lives in a neighboring, mostly rural, county. One day, he explained to me that people there give directions by saying, "Go to where Musselwhite's Grocery **used to be** and…" My thought was that I don't know where Musselwhite's **used to be**, so I'd be miserably lost. For several months, I have considered this and now realize there are several lessons here. First, knowing what **used to be** can be very valuable. Too many mistakes of the past are not learned and too many things that worked in the past are not used in the present. Charles also was using a wise method for teaching the unknown by using the known, since most people there knew where Musselwhite's **used to be**. Since I am running out of room, you take those three words and discover many more lessons. Coaches, educators, business leaders, parents, actually all of us, could better use what **used to be** to help us be what we ought to be.

But thanks be to God that, though you used to be slaves to sin, you have come to obey from your heart the pattern of teaching that has now claimed your allegiance. Romans 6:17 NIV

Tuesday - February 10, 2009

I recently did a "Custom Team Building" clinic for a high school team whose excellent theme for the season is: "Focus - Confidence - Finish." Today, let's explore the first word. I think that we all get distracted too much, but Ellen Langer, Harvard psychologist, says that we are not really **distracted**, but rather "we are **attracted** to something else." I often see that with people labeled as ADD or ADHD. The male student who has trouble paying attention in class will focus quite well when the right girl enters the room. Olympic Gold Medalist Michael Phelps (ADHD) seems to have few problems with focus while competing in the pool. These can be legitimate learning issues, but often a distraction is simply our choice. Let's focus on improving our choices of where and how long we focus, whether it is on the softball field, at the desk at work or school, behind the wheel, or sitting in church. Wisely choose where you are attracted.

Opportunities + Choices = Consequences   Bobby Simpson

Tuesday - February 17, 2009

Long ago, I bought booklets of 20 stamps and wondered why they had 21 slots, but only gave you 20 stamps. The last slot was a stamp-sized reminder that there were no more stamps…like I could not see that for myself! The postal service could get about a five percent better use of space by putting a stamp there. I've graduated to rolls of 100 self-adhesive stamps so I'm really not concerned with the 20 pack. Well, they have befuddled me again by often replacing the 100 roll with rolls of 50 state flag, double-sized stamps. Now, I have to get two rolls because someone decided to use twice as much space to get me my 100 stamps, plus the rolls seem stuck together with ultra-super glue and the price is going up again. To excel, coaches and players work to **use space better**. Check my office and you'll see I often do poorly, but let's all see if we can get a Higher Ground Stamp of Approval by improving use of the space that we have.

When they had all had enough to eat, he said to his disciples, "Gather the pieces that are left over. Let nothing be wasted." John 6:12 NIV

Tuesday - February 24, 2009

After seeing the story in my Sunday School book, I googled the name of John Stephen Akhwari. You may want to do the same and even watch the video. At the 1968 Olympics, he made the *greatest last place finish ever* as he ended the marathon an hour or so after the other runners. He had fallen earlier, whacked his head, been trampled, badly cut, and dislocated a knee. He got up, bandaged the knee and hobbled in pain to finish a grueling race. The medals and ceremony were all over when he arrived, but fans remaining gave him a thunderous ovation. The next day, a writer asked him why, with those injuries and no chance to win, did he finish the race. His reply was remarkable, "My country (Tanzania) did not send me 5000 miles to start a race. They sent me 5000 miles to finish one." When we encounter a quitting point, when challenged by frustration, confusion, fear, or fatigue, will we struggle, even if hobbling, and **finish the job**?

because you know that the testing of your faith develops perseverance. Perseverance must finish its work so that you may be mature and complete, not lacking anything. James 1:3-4 NIV

Tuesday - March 3, 2009

Graham Gano recently won the Lou Groza Award, given to the best kicker in NCAA football. A few months before winning the honor, the Florida State senior was not even sure that he would get to play last year. Just before the season started, Gano suffered a knee injury during practice and surgery was required. He came back in the third game, missed a 52-yard attempt on his first kick, then made 18 straight field goals, hit five 50 yards or longer, and had a 92.3 percent rate. I love his quote about the injury, "I think it helped me getting started off with the **basics** again." What an excellent example of **reframing** what seemed negative and wrapping it in positivism! Did you hear him? He said that the injury actually helped him. Could this message *gift wrapped* and sent to us suggest that we be careful about staying too long with the *fancy*? Should we remember the basic, common sense items and be sure they stay a major part of our efforts?

...out of weakness were made strong... Hebrews 11:34 NKJV

SPECIAL NOTICE: Just arrived – our 1st grandchild, Cullen Simpson Dunn **DOB** 02-27-09 **TOB** 4:03p.m. **Parents** Justin & Neilie Dunn **Wt** 7 lbs, 12.4 oz **Ht** 20.5 in **YOG** 2027 **Evaluation** Excellent hand/foot quickness & strength, decibel potential, *take charge* capability, and determination (measured during Early Boy Diaper Change Showcase), plus considered by several observers to be cutest, sweetest, most adorable, and most handsome male arrival in at least the last 50 years **Future Plans** Due to actual current and projected future early commitment trends, the family will accept athletic scholarship offers for approximately 60 days before advising Cullen on making a verbal commitment...leaning toward golf (Justin) or baseball (me), but open to all proposals.

Tuesday - March 10, 2009

When I conducted a "Team Building" clinic for BHP's softball team in South Carolina, Billy Anderson reminded me that I really needed to read *The Winner's Manual* by Jim Tressel, head football coach at Ohio State. In this terrific book, he says that the most rewarding introduction he ever had was when someone said, "Coach Tressel is a **dealer of hope**." That is quite a description, one that all of us should desire to wear. Karl Menninger defined hope as "an adventure, a going forward, a confident search for a rewarding life." On the softball field, at the job site, in the classroom, at home, or wherever we find ourselves, we should constantly encourage and inspire others to tackle the adventures and confidently press forward with hope as they move to higher ground in their lives. Please challenge yourself and others to move past wishful thinking and to acquire a depth of hope that allows a better future.

For I know the plans I have for you, declares the LORD, plans to prosper you and not to harm you, plans to give you hope and a future. Jeremiah 29:11 NIV

Tuesday - March 17, 2009

You may know that I took the name Higher Ground for our business from a hymn of the same name. The first verse talks about "pressing on the upward way," and our corporate name of Getting Better Every Day, Inc. emphasizes that same concept. The idea is to press upward, climb higher, get better, and move forward. A few weeks ago, I read a very catchy paragraph in a Sunday School lesson (*Explore The Bible*; LifeWay) that said, "Our eyes look forward; our ears face forward; our feet point forward. Although we are able to slide sideways or step backward if we choose, our usual movement is to go forward." Yes, externally we are designed to move forward. Internally, we are also designed to move forward to a higher level. In practice and games, at your job, in your relationships, what are you doing to propel yourself in the right direction? Plan your changes so that they add up to the proper **forward** movement. It's your choice.

And the LORD *said to Moses, "Why do you cry to Me? Tell the children of Israel to go forward."* Exodus 14:15 NKJV

Tuesday - March 24, 2009

Lately, I spent several days in the hospital. Thankfully, I was just observing. First, the husband of Christie Leger, our office manager, was in a serious fall, with lots of fractures and time in a trauma center and ICU (he's doing well). Then, my daughter gave birth to Cullen, the consensus best grandson ever born (I'm not the least bit biased). As I sat in her room, I pondered what thought could be filtered from all my time in those hospitals. The result was, "Learn to stay out of the way." My son-in-law, Justin, said that is his biggest problem when he plays golf. I saw lots of people who had that problem at the hospital. I constantly see good softball players severely limit their physical skills by letting their weaker mental skills get in the way. And, coaches frequently get in a player's way by forced cloning which retards athletic freedom. I am trying hard to intelligently **stay out of the way** more often. You have a personal invitation to join me.

Jesus said, "Let the little children come to me, and do not hinder them, for the kingdom of heaven belongs to such as these." Matthew 19:14 NIV

Tuesday - March 31, 2009

When I speak to coaches or business groups about "Team Preparation" or "Practice Organization," I use a simple two-word phrase to explore the **resources** that are available to us. *I STEP* reminds me to frequently consider the critical components of **I**nformation, **S**pace, **T**ime, **E**quipment, and **P**eople. Using this phrase, we can follow a simple, practical, and powerful framework for planning a practice, a project, or a strategy. Where do we get proper information and what part of it needs to be used today? How can we better use our facility or space to improve? What's the best manner of using the time that we have available? There is never enough of it...compress it so results are expanded. What can be used as equipment and how can it be used more creatively? Since the most powerful *P* in the whole *planning pod* is people, how can we maximize their contribution to the process? Consider taking a step up and make better use of *I STEP* **resources**.

But as it is written: "Eye has not seen, nor ear heard, Nor have entered into the heart of man The things which God has prepared for those who love Him." 1 Corinthians 2:9 NKJV

Tuesday - April 7, 2009

Jack Welch, former CEO of General Electric, and his wife Suzy send a *Weekly Welch* item via email. The February 18 article went to Jeff Couper, CFO of J.T. Turner Construction in Savannah, Georgia. He sent a copy to Tripp Turner, their Director of Business Development, who kindly sent it to me. It mentioned an interview with Chelsey "Sully" Sullenberger, the pilot who landed Flight 1549 in the Hudson River. When he was asked if he ever feared "not making it," he replied, "No, I knew I could do it." Let me make some quick points. First, on the front end of an activity (at-bat, presentation, test, interview), we should use positive visualization and self-talk, rather than say "I'll try my best," which just gives us a built-in excuse to fail. Next, confidence and conceit are not identical. Plus, Welch added, "…leaders undermine success by talking about the **risk of failure**." Finally, like Jeff and Tripp, help others by sharing good stuff.

So we may boldly say: "The Lord is *my helper; I will not fear. What can man do to me?"* Hebrews 13:6 NKJV

Tuesday - April 14, 2009

While coaching the British National Fastpitch Team a few years ago, I spent quite a bit of time riding the underground (subway). At each station, they always made a safety announcement, "**Mind the gap**," reminding us to be careful of the gap between the train and the platform in the station. Today, in education, I keep reading and hearing a reminder that we should seek to narrow the gap between average achievement scores for various sub-groups. In England, the advice was very logical and quite helpful. In education or other fields, though possibly well intended, the advice is illogical and often quite harmful. Narrowing a gap between students, athletes, employees, or other groups brings the masses closer to the average, which limits the higher levels of excellence. A much better goal would be to narrow the gap between what each individual or team is and what it could be. Determine today to mind the proper gap!

From God's point of view, the greatest waste in life is the gap between what you are and what you could be. David Jeremiah in *Life Wide Open*

Tuesday - April 21, 2009

Just minutes after I decided to use this topic, the mother of a college bound baseball player commented that her son seems to frequently be in the position where he thinks that he's got to get a hit. Today, consider how just changing one letter can make a huge difference. About 15 years ago, Rev. Shep Johnson said to think *get to* instead of *got to*. Instead of saying, "I've got to get a hit," try eagerly saying, "I get to get a hit!" Command versus opportunity! Replace the morning's groggy, "I got to get up," with a thankful, "I get to get up today!" Some people cannot get out of bed.

Instead of saying, "I've got to go to school" or "I've gotta go to church this morning," realize that in some countries people are not even allowed to go to school or church. Cherish that right. Remember to be thankful that you get to go to work, and stop complaining that you have got to go to work. Some do not have jobs. We get to choose – **got to or get to?**

Therefore, as we have opportunity, let us do good to all people, especially to those who belong to the family of believers. Galatians 6:10 NIV

Tuesday - April 28, 2009

Recently, I read that an education guru toting a doctorate stated that two of her six guiding principles were, "Each of us has a unique brain," and a quote by psychologist Alfred Adler, "What's best for the best is best for all." Then, I had a discussion with a multi-year Division I NCAA Softball All-American who was told that the way she hit in college was wrong. The educator's statements are conflicting and mimic the cloning efforts in sports, business, education, and other fields. If we are **unique**, then what is best for the best is not necessarily best for the rest. The swing that works for Jessica Mendoza, Crystl Bustos, or Alex Rodriguez is not necessarily going to work for your players. You do not likely have those same players on your team. If so, thank God and get out of the way. And, that All-American did quite well the wrong way, didn't she? *I ain't you and you ain't me*…bad English, but good truth. Please personalize!

I will praise You, for I am fearfully and wonderfully made; Marvelous are Your works, And that my soul knows very well. Psalm 139:14 NKJV

Tuesday - May 5, 2009

In recent years, I have helped young players learn to **mind their own business**. I used to think that was a negative phrase until I saw it used to mean that we should focus on what we should be doing instead of other things. Used that way, it means to avoid becoming entangled in things we shouldn't so that we are more effective at the things we should be doing. So, softball players need to get in the batter's box or pitcher's circle and get their mind fully focused on their own business. Likewise, some employees should pay complete attention to doing their job with excellence instead of being bogged down in office politics. Coaches can also improve with more focus on the performance of their job and less "business minding" related to umpires. As I heard a very wise mother tell her young child, we need to "tend to our own little red wagon." Seeking to *Get Better Every Day*, let's check whose business we mind and which red wagon we tend.

And in fact, you do love all of God's family throughout Macedonia. Yet we urge you, brothers and sisters, to do so more and more, and to make it your ambition to lead a quiet life: You should mind your own business and work with your hands, just as we told you, so that your daily life may win the respect of outsiders and so that you will not be dependent on anybody.
1 Thessalonians 4:10-12 NIV

Tuesday - May 12, 2009

A kind friend got me an advance copy of a very good read, *The Talent Code*, by bestseller author Daniel Coyle. Some was confusing and I disagreed at times, but was fascinated by what he found worldwide in talent development hotbeds for baseball, soccer, tennis, music, and art. He found that at least half of the top performers made progress through "small failures, a rhythmic pattern of botches." He saw "slow, fitful struggle ...seeking out the slippery hills...purposefully operating at the edges of their ability, so they would screw up." He describes "*deep practice*...struggling in certain targeted ways – operating at the edge of your ability, where you make mistakes – makes you smarter...experiences where you're forced to slow down, make errors, and correct them – as you would if you were walking up an ice-covered hill...end up making you swift and graceful." Seek **targeted struggle**, not blind thrashing, as you reach for success. Lots to think about...read.

We think of effortless performance as desirable, but it's really a terrible way to learn...Things that appear to be obstacles turn out to be desirable in the long haul. Robert Bjork, chair of psychology at UCLA (from *The Talent Code*).

Tuesday - May 19, 2009

Last week, I received a phone tree from our church. I jokingly emailed our associate pastor to ask if the tree needed to be watered. He then replied that I should both water and fertilize it. This silly electronic exchange reminded me that we each have roles to play and the fact that we often undervalue certain **roles** or attempt to place ourselves in an inappropriate role. I've even had an actress to come to one of our elite softball camps to help players improve in their role-playing skills and learn to adjust from being a hitter to becoming a fielder. What about you? Where you work, in your family, in relationships, or on your team, how well do you accept and play your role? Do you want to be the flower judge or are you willing to plant, water, or fertilize with excellence? Are you willing to be the assistant coach who should make suggestions or do you think you have to be the head coach and make decisions? **Roles** are critical…play your part well.

I planted the seed, Apollos watered it, but God made it grow.
1 Corinthians 3:6 NIV

Tuesday - May 26, 2009

I've told friends that I sometimes have trouble recognizing a former student when I see them outside a school setting. A few weeks ago, I was visiting my daughter's church in Savannah and her pastor told about a similar incident with a very famous violinist. He sat on the platform at a subway stop and played for about 45 minutes. During that time almost nobody even stopped to listen to him. At the end, he collected about $32 in tips, despite the fact that seats at his concert the night before averaged about $100 each. So often, we fail to recognize the outstanding if it's not in its normal setting. We can all become more aware of what is around us. Excellence may be sitting on the bench in the form of encouragement to a frustrated star. Heroism can be in a mother's hug, not just in typical places that we think of. Sales may come from a kind receptionist or quality carpenter, not just the salesman or architect. Improve **awareness and recognition**!

He was in the world, and though the world was made through him, the world did not recognize him. John 1:10 NIV

Tuesday - June 2, 2009

My 13-week old grandson Cullen recently showed me a very valuable lesson. He has this almost nightly routine of bath, bottle, swaddle, and bed. In case you don't know, **swaddling** is a very old practice of wrapping babies tightly in cloth or blankets and restricting their limbs. It lost favor in the 17th century, but modern medical studies indicate it helps some babies go to sleep, remain asleep, and may reduce risk of SIDS. Cullen went to his bed about 10:00, but by 3:00 had *unswaddled* one foot and verbally made it clear that he wanted some freedom. He peacefully slept in his mother's bed until she woke him at 7:30. Cullen very intelligently (in my unbiased opinion) reminded me that sometimes restrictions are good and sometimes freedom is needed. This definitely applies with many players who often need freedom from swaddling mechanics that restrict athleticism. Let's all improve choices about swaddling and freedom. Thanks, Cullen.

Therefore, since we are surrounded by such a great cloud of witnesses, let us throw off everything that hinders and the sin that so easily entangles. And let us run with perseverance the race marked out for us, Hebrews 12:1 NIV

Tuesday - June 9, 2009

On the day that I wrote this, I worked to teach a nine-year old softball player in Florida a habit to help her on defense. Seeing her pick up a ball with her glove, I made the point that if she picked it up with her bare hand that she could throw sooner and get it where it needed to be a little sooner. This could result in an out and maybe help win a game. The purpose of my instruction was to teach her the value of building habits while she was young. Actually, we really have very little to say about whether we create habits. However, we do get to make the very important choice whether we create good habits or bad habits. If we regularly pick up the ball with our glove during practice, we will increase the odds of doing that in a game. If we learn early and practice regularly doing it correctly, we develop a good habit for life. Pause and think about your life…are you building bad glove habits or good **bare hand habits**? Make your habits good ones.

Do not be deceived: "Evil company corrupts good habits." 1 Corinthians 15:33 NKJV

Tuesday - June 16, 2009

I believe it was Bill Lee who said that the way to get a hitter out is to throw the ball above, below, before, or after the bat. That means that he did not care how good a swing the hitter had if he could fool the hitter's eyes and get him to swing in the wrong place or at the wrong time. That is the art of deception, somewhat a way of counterfeiting the ball. When my daughter was in London, a salesman told her to be very careful where she set her *designer* purse, not knowing that it was not the real thing…it just looked like one. I have been told that law enforcement agents find counterfeit money, not so much by knowing what is counterfeit, but rather knowing the real thing so well that they realize something is different. So often, we get fooled by the pitch, the purse, or the money because we do not have a thorough enough knowledge or enough experience with the truth. May we all determine to better determine what is **real and true**.

And you shall know the truth, and the truth shall make you free. John 8:32 NKJV

Tuesday - June 23, 2009

Not too long ago, Paul DaCosta loaned me a book on DVD, *Paranoia and Power*, by Dr. Gene Landrum. Some interesting content from the book follows: Some who did not graduate from high school were Disney,

Picasso, Frank Lloyd Wright, and Mary Lou Retton (GED). Normal equals mediocrity. There can be a danger in knowing too much. You must change inside before you change outside. A kid in kindergarten laughs an average of 300 times a day...adults average just 17. Be what you are not, so you can become more than you would otherwise be. See the forest and the trees instead of saying that you cannot see the forest for the trees. Average creative ability retained at certain ages is estimated to be – 5 year olds (100%), 7 year olds (50%), 16 year olds (25%), and 40 year olds (1%). I hope at least one of these statements was **thought provoking** and helpful for you. If not, read them again and see what you can discover and use.

Woe to you, scribes and Pharisees, hypocrites! For you clean the outside of the cup and the plate, but inside they are full of greed and self-indulgence. Matthew 23:25 ESV

Tuesday - June 30, 2009

I recently read an article from the November/December, 2008 issue of *NSCAA Soccer Journal*, written by Dr. Jay Martin (Editor), expressing concern with elite young soccer **players who play but do not compete**. He states that we have "focused so much on playing, that we have not taught our players to compete – to fight – to work hard or to have the will to win." In many areas of sports, business, education, and life, we seem to emphasize skills and showing those skills, but we fail to teach enough about healthy battling, struggling, overcoming obstacles, and competing with ourselves and others. Research indicates that constant praise of innate intellectual or physical skill "can prevent young athletes/students from living up to their potential...studies show that teaching...to focus on effort rather than ability helps make them high achievers and competitors in school, on the field and in life." Will we apply that to our mentoring!

Players who PLAY bring skill; players who COMPETE bring everything. Ken Hitchcock NHL Coach

74 | THOUGHTS FOR TUESDAY

Most people mistake speed and skill for talent. Real talent STARTS with energy, drive, work ethic and the will to win. Without these attributes, a player can never be great. Allen Fox, author of *The Winners Mind*

Tuesday - July 7, 2009

I spend many hours helping athletes gain or maintain confidence. Without it, they lack trust and are very cautious and tentative in their actions, rather than decisive and powerful. Often, they are confused and think they cannot be both humble and confident. Ken Blanchard, co-author of *The One Minute Manager* (one of top management books of all time), insightfully explored **humility** in his 2005 book, *Lead Like Jesus*. He says, "…humility is a heart attitude that reflects a keen understanding of your limitations to accomplish something on your own. It gives credit to forces other than your own knowledge or effort…realizing and emphasizing the importance of others. It is not putting yourself down; it is lifting others up." He adds, "…people with humility don't think less of themselves; they just think of themselves less." Understand the essence of humility and realize that it can co-exist with confidence. Choose wisely and lift yourself and others.

Humble yourselves in the sight of the Lord, and He will lift you up. James 4:10 NKJV

Tuesday - July 14, 2009

I've read materials from a large number of leaders in various fields, but had never heard of Kop Kopmeyer until recently. Kopmeyer wrote four large books which each contained 250 success principles. Brian Tracy tells of asking him which of the thousand was the most important. With no hesitation, he answered, "Do what you should do, when you should do it, whether you feel like it or not." He then added, "There are 999 other success principles that I have found in my reading and experience, but without self-discipline, none of them work." Read that answer again! In a world where people base so much action or inaction on what they feel like doing instead of what should be done, or delay what should be done until they feel like it, Kopmeyer's advice is to be carefully heeded. He boldly stated that none of the wisest principles espoused by the most learned philosopher, teacher, coach, or other mentor will work without **self-discipline**.

To learn, you must love discipline; it is stupid to hate correction. Proverbs 12:1 NLT

Tuesday - July 21, 2009

I am sitting in an Atlanta hotel preparing for a team building session tomorrow for a local high school softball team. I just reread a comment by Patrick Lencioni, in *Overcoming the Five Dysfunctions of a Team*, where he says, "More than anything else, it (teamwork) comes down to courage and persistence." Yesterday, I taught a Sunday School lesson that emphasized endurance. So, I guess the topic today should deal with the concept of perseverance, endurance, persistence, stick-to-it-ness. I remember Jack Stallings, with whom I coached baseball at Florida State, saying, "Coaching is a lot like raising children; it's easy, but you have to do it **every day**." Far too often, people give in and get out instead of being willing daily to struggle, stick to it, fight, overcome obstacles, and claim victories in life's battles. As I pondered this today, a new word came to mind. I think all of us need to improve our *everydayness* skills. I like my new word and I plan to work at it daily. I invite you to join me.

To those who by persistence in doing good seek glory, honor and immortality, he will give eternal life. But for those who are self-seeking and who reject the truth and follow evil, there will be wrath and anger. Romans 2:7-8 NIV

Tuesday - July 28, 2009

Recently, the Atlanta Braves retired Greg Maddux's jersey. Looking through some old items, I found some 1998 comments by Maddux in *The Atlanta Constitution*. Questioned about his future enshrinement into baseball's Hall of Fame, he replied, "I'm not history yet. I'm not *past tense* yet, so I don't think about it. It's not so much what I've accomplished, so much as **what more can I do**? I don't want to see (what I've accomplished) until I'm done. I'm aware I've had some pretty special years. I'm also aware it doesn't matter. It's not going to help me win my next game. I'm not concerned about where I'm heading at all. If you ask me what I'll be doing 10 years from now, I have no idea…I understand the expectations on me are as heavy as on anyone. My way of dealing with it is not to let it bother me, which is easier said than done. I appreciate (what I've done) every day, but I don't get caught up in it." Maddux used his past for confidence, but wisely kept it in perspective.

Brothers, I do not consider that I have made it my own. But one thing I do: forgetting what lies behind and straining forward to what lies ahead, I press on toward the goal for the prize of the upward call of God in Christ Jesus. Let those of us who are mature think this way, and if in anything you think otherwise, God will reveal that also to you. Philippians 3:13-15 ESV

Tuesday - August 4, 2009

One of my most favorite softball people is Sue Enquist. She holds more National Championships (11) than anyone in the history of college softball, retiring at UCLA in 2006 after 27 years, with a record of 887-175-1, plus 65 All-Americans and 12 Olympians. A few days ago, I needed her change of address and her email reply had a simple, yet powerful, message. With her permission, I share part of it. "Loving life and keeping busy. Camps and clinics. Corporate speaking. Consulting Reese Witherspoon on a movie next year. Title IX expert witness, 1-0 in cases thus far." The next line then reminded me of one of her special qualities…her willingness, despite her status and very busy schedule, to always have time for people, "When Dad passed late year, I moved in to take care of mama E. She is doing great at 84." We all get busy and we seem to have so much to do, but let's all determine to take more **time for others**. Sue does…so can we.

She opens her mouth with wisdom, And on her tongue is the law of kindness. She watches over the ways of her household, And does not eat the bread of idleness. Her children rise up and call her blessed;…
Proverbs 31:26-28 NKJV

Tuesday - August 11, 2009

2001 Greek National Team outfielder Elina Farantou stood with me on a field in Holland. With little confidence, frustrated, and teary-eyed, she asked when she would see success from all of her hard work and preparation. That team had almost no softball experience and it was difficult to continue preparing and not see rewards. I told her that I was convinced she would succeed, but I did not know when it would happen. The day she hit her first line drive shot to the outfield, her eyes at first base met my eyes in the dugout and the huge smiles on each face matched. My friend in the U.S. was rapidly promoted to a position when another worker left the company. He had not prepared himself for that day and soon was replaced. Elina used her softball preparation and is a confident married lady in Greece. My friend in the U.S. learned his lesson, prepared well, and is a very successful business owner. Do we just want rewards or are we **willing to prepare**?

It's not the will to win, but the will to prepare to win that makes the difference. Bear Bryant, late University of Alabama football coach

Tuesday - August 18, 2009

Our pastor, Jim Duggan, alerted me to the Scoville Chile Heat Chart, developed by Wilbur Scoville in 1912 to rate the heat level of various chile peppers. The ratings go from 0 for mildest to 10 for hottest. Sweet Bells have a rating of 0 (negligible Scoville units), Jalapeno rate a 4 (2500-5000 units), Cayenne are a 7 (30,000-50,000 units), Habanero are a 9 (350,000 –575,000 units), and Indian Tezpur are a 10, with up to 1,000,000 units. For us to be successful in sports or life, we need to apply this in two ways. First, we need to be able to "stand the heat" when we are challenged to compromise or abandon solid values or principles. Second, we need a hot passion for a mission so that we can commit, endure struggles, overcome obstacles, and hang in there until victory eventually comes. Let's determine to have an Indian Tezpur **heat resistance** level, plus the same level **passion** for truth and success, as we strive to *Get Better Every Day*.

If you have fire in your heart, we can put what you need in your head.
Charles Wang

So, because you are lukewarm—neither hot nor cold—I am about to spit you out of my mouth. Revelations 3:16 NIV

Tuesday - August 25, 2009

Only a few of you have ever heard of the late Rod Blaylock. He served for many years as the recreation director in Albany, Georgia, and was well known by those involved in softball and square dancing. Rod was a district commissioner with me in the 1980's, when I served as the state commissioner for ASA Softball. He puzzled us at state meetings when he would make a motion and, after all the discussion, then vote against his own motion. Actually, we could learn a lot from his actions. His original heartfelt motion got a much-needed discussion started. He was willing to listen to that discussion, carefully consider all the information, and then have the courage to face the facts and take the correct action by reversing himself. It takes guts to admit a mistake in our coaching or playing, our job, our relationships, or other area of life and then correct it. Often, we stubbornly defend our mistake. **Flip-flops** like Rod's teach us a better way.

If we confess our sins, He is faithful and just to forgive us our sins and to cleanse us from all unrighteousness. 1 John 1:9 NKJV

Tuesday - September 1, 2009

The recent Sunday School lesson and the golf book that I was reading to help me teach softball both talked about *need*. Working with hitters, I often get deep into the time between pitches. What should she do in the 15-20 seconds to help her when she gets back in the box? Bottom line, she should personalize that pre-time based on her needs once she enters the box. Employ *backward chaining* to discover the proper actions. Maybe we should do that in education. Look backward from the *real world* and ask what is needed most for proper entry. Then, we might emphasize respect for self and others, personal responsibility, and strong work ethic instead of only cramming in logarithms, past participles, Tin Pan Alley, and mitochondria. In daily life, maybe we could help people learn to struggle instead of enabling bad habits. Let's take a transforming look at **needs**.

Then Jesus called a little child to Him, set him in the midst of them, and said, "Assuredly, I say to you, unless you are converted and become as little children, you will by no means enter the kingdom of heaven." Matthew 18:2-3 NKJV

Tuesday - September 8, 2009

A few Sundays ago, my daughter was at our house in Tifton and she received a very short text from a co-worker who was in Savannah. It simply said, "**Great Is Thy Faithfulness**." Her smile told me that it had a special meaning. She and her co-worker both grew up in Baptist churches and now attend the same Methodist church in Savannah. The two denominations have very close theology and I actually grew up in a Methodist church and now am Baptist. The message was simply telling my daughter that they had sung a very traditional Baptist song in their Methodist church that day. It also reminds us that a short message can say a lot...the past can help us with the present and the future, plus we should often check our level of faithfulness. Are we faithful to our religious commitments, as well as faithful to our team, our employer, our family, and our relationships? How faithful are we to solid principles and proper actions? Just four words!!

Through the LORD's mercies we are not consumed, Because His compassions fail not. They are new every morning; Great is Your faithfulness. Lamentations 3:22-23 NKJV

Tuesday - September 15, 2009

I first saw her years ago as a thin 12-year old at one of our softball camps. A few years later, while conducting a large clinic at a high school, I discovered that she played there. While talking to her coach a year or so later, I asked about the girl and was told that she was her *but girl*. The coach said that she resisted change and would always use the word *but* in replies to the coach's suggestions for improvement. She might say that she could do something, but then offer a reason not to (e.g. *I could change that footwork, but I think I can do it better my way*). Definitely, that can frustrate a coach and also impede skill improvement. What about you? Are you a *but person*? Do you use the word too much and impede progress on the field, the job, or in personal relationships? Count the times you use it today. By the way, the girl changed her approach to learning, starred at a major DI school, and is now a successful college coach. We can **change**!

Listen, my sons, to a father's instruction; pay attention and gain understanding. I give you sound learning, so do not forsake my teaching. Proverbs 4:1-2 NIV

Tuesday - September 22, 2009

When I went to a high school tournament last week, John Pinson's email directions to the fields in Baconton, Georgia, included "one intersection beyond a fairly new country store that closed but is now being reopened…turn into pecan grove." Later, he rephrased "go to store that is or is not there anymore, go thru a pecan grove." Fortunately, in early morning light, I spotted the *is* or *is not* store, made the turn, and enjoyed a terrific day at the fields in the pecan grove. It struck me that much of softball and much of life are about ***used to be's*** and ***gonna be's***. The country store used to be open and is gonna be open again. How did you used to do things in the past? How are you gonna do things in the future? Should you change what you used to do? Is there a better way that you are gonna use? Carefully consider your ***used to be's*** and ***gonna be's***. Let's determine that our ***gonna be's*** are gonna be better than our ***used to be's***. *Get Better Every Day*!

They named it Dan after their ancestor Dan, who was born to Israel—though the city used to be called Laish. Judges 18:29 NIV

Tuesday - September 29, 2009

In May 2003, in preparation for an Olympic Qualifier tournament in Italy, I sent an email to the British Women's Fastpitch Softball National Team that I was coaching. A slightly modified form follows and applies to each of us in the roles we play in life. "**Expect to be surprised**. I know for a fact that I will receive surprises while in Italy…possibly sooner. A bus will be late, a game time or field will be changed, an injury will occur, a meal may be missed, a player's performance will be better or worse than expected, or a reaction to someone's words or actions will be totally shocking. Any or all of these will happen. Expect to be surprised in both softball and personal matters. In either, your job is to expect it and then adjust appropriately. If you can't cope with change, surprise, and adjustment, then you should not be on this team. It's that simple. Surprise is an integral part of championship softball and your ability to adjust is critical to being successful."

Beloved, do not be surprised at the fiery trial when it comes upon you to test you, as though something strange were happening to you. 1 Peter 4:12 ESV

Tuesday - October 6, 2009

If you go to the website for the Mill Creek HS Softball Team (Hoschton, GA), you'll see a section entitled, "In the dugout with." When you go in the dugout with Coach Kelly Murdock, you'll see a very interesting first item in her "Favorite things about Mill Creek Softball." You see, item number one is **goals and gratitudes**. Kelly has been the AAA Player of the Year, AAAAA Coach of the Year, spoken at the Italian National Clinic, and her program is always one of the best in the state. Many successful people like her emphasize goals, but at Mill Creek practices, Kelly and her players always take time to discuss what they are grateful for. It's what Zig Ziglar calls a *gratitude attitude*. Like Ziglar recommends, Kelly has all the Lady Hawks learning to say "thank you," instead of today's frequent "I'm entitled...I'm owed...I'm due." Today, as we reach for goals, let's follow the lessons of Kelly Murdock and Zig Ziglar and be truly grateful.

Passionate people who have an attitude of gratitude...see everything in life as being a gift from the hand of a good and loving God. They take nothing for granted and give thanks for everything. Zig Ziglar in *Better Than Good*

Tuesday - October 13, 2009

Dave Farrington wrote a 2004 book with a superb title, *More Bricks, Less Straw*. Based on Pharaoh's response to Moses in Exodus 5, it tackles the issue of getting **more done with less** resources and getting it done "better, faster, and cheaper." Whether we are coaching, playing, teaching, running a business, managing a family, or any number of other tasks, this seems to be a challenge that all of us face. Farrington mentions eight keys to success in this venture, one being effective **communication**. He wisely states, "The timing of a message affects the listener's understanding and acceptance of it." I frequently see a terrific swing fail because it is taken at the wrong time or a great pitch gets blasted because it is thrown at the wrong time. Likewise, many fantastic messages get delivered at the wrong time, having a negative effect when they could have been so helpful. Think again about what you are going to say. Is now the best time to say it?

"Therefore go now and work; for no straw shall be given you, yet you shall deliver the quota of bricks." Exodus 5:18 NKJV

Tuesday - October 20, 2009

Fascinated by *so-called small things*, it's no surprise that I just read *The Power Of Small*, written by Linda Kaplan Thaler and Robin Koval. Ponder and use some of their following suggestions to do big things in your life: Instead of changing your look, change your outlook. Remember *please*, *thank you*, and handwritten notes. "The next time someone shares an anecdote...ask a question before you launch into your own tale." The janitor at a San Diego hotel came up with the idea of outside elevators. "What you ignore becomes more." The very successful Aflac duck and ad theme came about during a goofing-off moment. Research shows conversation skills are more important in business than GPA. Try an "e-mail diet day" inside your office. "Take the first small step; And then keep on walking." It's a very short book (133 small pages) about **so-called small things**, but reading it can make a big difference in sports, business, education, and life.

If you think small things don't matter, try spending the night in a room with a mosquito. The Dalai Lama

Tuesday - October 27, 2009

Nicole Wessels was a scrappy little infielder when I worked with the Dutch National Softball Team. During that time, she came to play with the junior college in my hometown. One thing that puzzled her was the custom of people to walk by her and ask, "**How are you doing**?" She would stop to tell them how she was doing, but they just kept walking, not seeming to care about the answer. This is more than a social custom, especially when we extend it a little. We should definitely ask others what they think and then we should caringly pay close attention. Whether it's a nation's president asking a general, corporate executive asking a secretary, store manager asking a clerk, head coach asking an assistant or a player, administrator surveying teachers, or parent asking a child, let's all get better at asking and then paying attention to what is said. Let's refuse to physically or mentally *walk on by* without using a terrific opportunity to learn.

I don't care how much you know until I know how much you care.

The way of a fool seems right to him, but a wise man listens to advice.
Proverbs 12:15 NIV

Tuesday - November 3, 2009

In the fall of my sophomore year in college, I took *Fundamentals of Speech* and Dr. Whitehead was quite a creative instructor. During a session on extemporaneous speech, he would call us to the front of the class, then toss out such topics as "Uses Of Ear Wax" or "Ways To Use Peach Fuzz." For my topic, he asked me to describe the sound of one hand clapping! Fortunately, my gray matter kicked in, reminding me of a popular song by Simon and Garfunkel. I quickly stated, "It's the 'Sound of Silence,'" sat down, and got his smile and my A. Not only was it a good reply to his request, it is also good advice for many of us today. As one who likes to talk a lot, I know I often need to speak less and listen more. I imagine many of you are people of action who may need to often pause and preview, feeding forward a solid philosophical and practical plan, and pause again after an action to review and reflect on the feedback. Oh, the value of **timely silence**!!

Lord, keep your arm around my shoulder and your hand over my mouth.
Sign in gift shop at St. Mary's Hospital in Athens, Georgia

Tuesday - November 10, 2009

Brent Strom, a friend who instructs in pro baseball, presents concepts that often challenge others. Many of his ideas are beyond the curve of what is normally taught (e.g. pitchers first learning to throw like infielders, using golf stances to help players get more power). Creative mavericks often find their ideas rejected. This parallels the words of Gordon MacKenzie, Hallmark's former Creative Paradox. In *Orbiting The Giant Hairball* (recommended by my daughter, Neilie), he says, "when one of us finds the courage to grow…to leave the status quo of the Hairball…that can be pretty threatening for the rest of us to witness. The threat is that we, too, might be expected to grow. And sometimes growing can be a frightening and painful experience…So we contrive to stop others in our loop who display a desire and willingness to grow." I greatly admire Brent's creativity, determination, and growth. Will we have the same **courage to grow**?

Every school I visited was participating in the suppression of creative genius. Gordon MacKenzie

Tuesday - November 17, 2009

They say it's really good for us, but I hate milk. The last glass of milk that I drank was when I was about twelve, which is a long time ago. I may use it with cereal, but not by itself. However, I absolutely love ice cream. First of all, it tastes fantastic. In addition, it is one of a small number of items that talks to me from inside the refrigerator. Celery, carrots, and broccoli never yell at me, but I frequently hear ice cream call me to come visit. Once I arrive, it asks me to place it in a bowl and the rest is delicious history. Well, recently one of my favorite coaches used ice cream in another, very constructive way. A teenage pitcher and her father were so discouraged by her practice session that my friend told them that they would all skip the next physical workout. Instead they would meet locally for ice cream and discuss her goals and an effective approach for achievement. What a yummy reminder of the value of **smart work** in addition to hard work!

I scream, you scream, we all scream for ice cream. Childhood chant

Tuesday - November 24, 2009

Before self-service gas, we told someone to *fill 'er up*. Bonnie and I just spent some time alone with Cullen, our 8 ½ month old grandson, in his home. Saturday was a *fill 'er up* day, as special as any day I've ever had, and I've been across the USA and a dozen nations, coached in Olympic stadiums, and done clinics with major leaguers. This day was all about Cullen, watching him learn and love life. For me…a donut, 2 sandwiches, soup, a little ice cream. I learned a toy train travels on its side or top. It doesn't need wheels. He pulled up constantly, always studying and finding a safe way down. He always got from where he was to where he wanted to be. No matter where I put him, he always crawled to the kitchen. He taught how energizing a smile (or 500 smiles) can be. It was extreme simplicity and deep joy. Can we transfer lessons from a precious little boy and have *fill 'er up* days as we coach players, work jobs, and enrich relationships?

And the disciples were filled with joy and with the Holy Spirit. Acts 13:52 NKJV

Tuesday - December 1, 2009

About a year ago, I was lying down getting over some minor surgery, wrapped up in the surfing power of a TV remote control, when I stopped to watch an interview of an American soldier in Afghanistan. When he was asked how he saw his purpose, he said that he'd say it like he told his little girl when he left home, "take care of as many good people as he could, get rid of as many bad people as he could, and bring as many of his people home as he could." She said, "Okay." A lesson from his concise words is that we constantly need to more effectively define, commit to, and accomplish the proper purpose in all areas of our life. Actions should rarely be random. As an instructor, I am constantly asking players to tell me the purpose of the upcoming or just completed swing. How well do we **ask, define, commit, and accomplish the proper purpose** at our desk, in our home, in our relationships? Let's all seek to improve at our everyday purposes.

But He said to them, "Let us go into the next towns, that I may preach there also, because for this purpose I have come forth." Mark 1:38 NKJV

Tuesday - December 8, 2009

I often emphasize how critical energy and passion are in our quest for excellence. Unfortunately, I see far too many people, even athletes, that we could classify as *oxygen thieves* or *energy leaks*. Some just seem to drift through life as clouds drift across the sky. So, I ask you to please not underestimate the value I place on passion for the task. I received an email recently that reminded me that mixed with the heat of a passionate drive, we must maintain a cool calm and control. I actually spend only a little time watching sports on TV…a lot of time actively involved, but just a little TV time. However, I seemed to have watched a lot of college football lately and it has been very evident that the energy and passion is there, but far too often the **calm and control** is absent. As we journey toward excellence in sports, business, education, or relationships, please stoke the fires of passion, but remember to do so with calm and control.

Let me do nothing today without calmness of soul. Words of John Wesley, sent by Tom Draffin.

Tuesday - December 15, 2009

It was in the fifth or sixth grade (been awhile, so not sure) that I won the school spelling bee. Even today, I spell well, but one word that has trouble getting the letters just right as it travels the path from my brain to my fingers or lips is **persevere**. I looked it up to get it correct this time, but I often put in an extra letter and get it wrong. Maybe spelling the word has some importance, but actually living the word has a whole lot more impact. So many players want to give up too soon. They quit too easily. Many are very close to succeeding, but just do not put in enough repetitions to get it right. The same is true for far too many in business, education, marriage, government, and other areas where people are unwilling to struggle through the swamp to get to solid ground. We unfortunately complain too much, quit too soon, and accept failure or seek a bailout. Spell it wrong if you must, but please determine today to live it right. Success could be very, very close.

Many of life's failures are people who did not realize how close they were to success when they gave up. Thomas Edison

Tuesday - December 22, 2009

When my daughter was a teenager, my wife asked her if she wanted to work for me during the CHRISTmas holidays so that she could make a little money. Neilie replied, "*I don't need to work…I've got $16.00 and a half a tank of gas.*" Life, at least for her at that moment, was simple. I write quite often about simplicity so that I can remind myself (I can be a slow learner at times, so repetition is needed) to boil softball skills down to the core. We can get so bogged down in feet, elbows, shoulders, hands, and other body parts that we forget the core of hitting is seeing well and attacking violently a little ball with the stick we hold. The preaching of phase 1, 2, 3, and more can cause a *skillectomy* (word not familiar to dictionary writers) and remove our athleticism and reduce our performance. Whatever it is that you are doing or teaching others to do, keep in mind that ***$16.00 and a half a tank of gas*** may be all that you need to succeed.

Today in the town of David a Savior has been born to you; he is Christ the Lord. Luke 2:11 NIV

Tuesday - December 29, 2009

Long ago, Jack Stallings, for whom I had been an assistant baseball coach at Florida State, came to help the Tifton Tomboys, a girls' slowpitch team that won six ASA Nationals in ten years. He went back to Georgia Southern, telling the softball coach that he saw the best shortstop, baseball or softball, that he had seen all year. Darby Cottle Veazey, my niece, later played at Florida State, winning the Broderick Award as the nation's best player. This past October 28, Darby's son Chance, a freshman baseball player who had won the starting job at second base for the University of Georgia, was in an accident that paralyzed him below the waist. As we leave one year and enter another, my thought is to encourage you to **cry, laugh, reflect, and be inspired**. NOTE: Please watch a terrific 6-minute ESPN video (2017) of Chance and his long friendship with Alex Wood and Kyle Farmer, players with the L.A. Dodgers at the time of the filming. Google Chance Veazey for more inspiring items.

http://www.espn.com/watch/player?id=21005594&lang=en

*For I know the thoughts that I think toward you, says the L*ORD*, thoughts of peace and not of evil, to give you a future and a hope.* Jeremiah 29:11 NKJV (This verse was selected by Chance Veazey)

THOUGHTS FOR TUESDAY
GOLD MEDAL WISDOM FOR LIFE

2010

Get **wisdom**! Get understanding! Do not forget, nor turn away from the words of my mouth. Do not forsake her, and she will preserve you; Love her, and she will keep you. **Wisdom** is the principal thing; Therefore get **wisdom**. And in all your getting, get understanding (emphasis added). Proverbs 4:5-7 NKJV

Tuesday - January 5, 2010

In 1927, a relative named Hallie Erminie Rives (Rives was my mother's middle name; my second grandson is named Ryves from an alternate family spelling) wrote *The Magic Man*. It was one of many books she authored and my wife has always, with repeated failure, wanted me to read it. I almost never read novels, but did recently thumb through it looking for something to jump off a page. Well, on page 285, one character said, "Oh, you presume! You presume too much!" That's the truth. We presume that hitters have to fix swings to get better, when often they simply need to "get their head straight." We presume if a great player does it a certain way, then our players need to do it that way. We presume that things that sound good are good. We presume that new is better than old. We presume that high-tech pictures don't lie. Oh, we **presume** way too much.

And do not presume to say to yourselves, 'We have Abraham as our father,' for I tell you, God is able from these stones to raise up children for Abraham. Matthew 3:9 ESV

Tuesday - January 12, 2010

Long ago, Jake Gaither spoke to a graduate class I attended at Florida State. A very colorful, very wise, and very successful football coach at Florida A&M University, he certainly did not disappoint us that evening. When asked what he looked for in a player, he replied, "I like them **agile, mobile, and hostile**." To get the right effect, let each of those words end with a sound like the word *style*. After some thought, I realized that, properly defined and applied, these qualities can help all of us. A dictionary and thesaurus tell me that *agile* can mean ready to act, alert, or swift. *Mobile* means movable, portable…what I would say about someone willing to change a strategy or method when necessary. *Hostile* can certainly have some negative meanings, but it also means aggressive and smart aggressiveness has helped many an athlete and a multitude of people in other areas. Coach Gaither, thanks for the words of wisdom that we still can use today.

Be alert and of sober mind. Your enemy the devil prowls around like a roaring lion looking for someone to devour. 1 Peter 5:8 NIV

Tuesday - January 19, 2010

I regularly take notes while listening to someone speak and quite often those notes lead me to a topic different than the one chosen by the speaker, even if I am enjoying those comments. I guess I'm guilty of *multi-noting*. Speaking fairly often to groups about **leadership**, my off-topic notes turned recently in that direction. Three thoughts I had were (1) Good leaders quickly stop dwelling on what they don't have and take stock of what they do have and how they can best use it to accomplish their mission; (2) Good leaders realize that it is better to look bad doing something that is right than to look good doing something that is wrong; (3) Good leaders have the courage to decommit if their commitment was made to something that is wrong. They realize that the direction of a flip-flop determines its correctness and value. Remember that each of us (coach, player, employer, employee, parent, child) leads somebody (ourselves or others). Lead well!

Then Peter said, "Silver and gold I do not have, but what I do have I give you: In the name of Jesus Christ of Nazareth, rise up and walk." Acts 3:6 NKJV

Tuesday - January 26, 2010

At our recent SUPER Clinic, Jaime Wohlbach spent a lot of time showing advanced catchers and coaches how the positioning of the body, as well as the mitt, can be used in conjunction with the plate umpire's angle to make a ball look like a strike or a strike look like a ball. She did an excellent job demonstrating how angles affect the picture of the pitch and it reminded me of the often-quoted myth that "Pictures don't lie." The **integrity of a picture**, just like that of statistics, often depends on the angle from which the picture was taken. Many an actor or actress looks taller, shorter, thinner, or plumper based on camera angle. Likewise, to effectively use a visual image of a hitter or the explanation of a concept in business, industry, or education, we better know the angle of the presentation. Maybe the picture does not lie, but the angle, interpretation, or application can all definitely lead to major errors. See accurately, analyze well, use wisely.

And the Lord *God said to the woman, "What is this you have done?" The woman said, "The serpent deceived me, and I ate."* Genesis 3:13 NKJV

Tuesday - February 2, 2010

While coaching the British Women's Fastpitch National Team (2001-2004), I sought to operate on about a dozen "Key Principles For Consideration." These were the core items that I used to guide the program and the eighth one on the list recently came to mind. It simply stated, "Think and act with *If...Then* rather than **What If**.*"* So often, athletes, and many others, allow doubt, fear, confusion, and other emotions to defensively wonder, "What if this or that occurs?" For example, the hitter might ask, "What if she throws me another wicked low, outside drop?" With that fearful, questioning approach come a defensive posture and distinct disadvantage to the hitter. Instead, we sought an offensive approach and told ourselves, "**If** she throws a wicked low, outside drop, **then** I am going to recognize it early and hit a shot to the opposite field." Likewise, YOU can confidently take charge of a situation and plan what to do IF a certain thing occurs.

Is not the whole land before you? Please separate from me. If you take the left, then I will go to the right; or, if you go to the right, then I will go to the left." Genesis 13:9 NKJV

Tuesday - February 9, 2010

I've emphasized sports vision for a very long time, ever since I worked with the Royals Baseball Academy. During the first week a young hitter was in pro baseball, our only instructions were, "See the ball well." That is much different than the typical advice of "Watch the ball" or "Keep your eye on the ball." Those are both well meant, but less-than-effective phrases. How many meetings or classes have you attended where you "kept your eye on the speaker," but did not really learn anything visually? How many times have you "watched the TV," but had to ask someone what just happened? In hitting and in life, we need to improve our visual study skills, increase visual collection of information in terms of choice, accuracy, and completeness, and then properly apply the information we gather. Decide today to study the pitch (recognize *where* and *when* it will arrive) and likewise apply that skill to **see** people and places **well** today.

Turn your eyes upon Jesus, **look full** *in His wonderful face, and the things of earth will grow strangely dim in the light of His glory and grace* (emphasis added). "Turn Your Eyes Upon Jesus," by Helen H. Lemmel, 1922.

Tuesday - February 16, 2010

Debbie Brown, a fellow teacher, recently won a local *Biggest Losers* contest for her age division. I really admire her intense commitment to a purpose and was delighted that she won. It was kinda interesting to say that she won due to a loss (weight). Steve Clarfield, co-author of *Best of the Best – Women's Fast Pitch Softball*, is a clinical psychologist who has talked to me about what he calls "Learning Losses and Lazy Losses." If players already "know everything" or put themselves in positions where they easily win, they set themselves up for lazy losses. Even a win could possibly be termed a long term loss. He states, "Focus on learning to be a player, no matter the outcome on the scoreboard, and you teach the child to enjoy the journey wherever it takes her." Let's all take a close look at wins and losses and see if they are best described as **lazy or learning**.

Consider it pure joy, my brothers and sisters, whenever you face trials of many kinds, because you know that the testing of your faith produces perseverance. Let perseverance finish its work so that you may be mature and complete, not lacking anything. James 1:2-4 NIV

Tuesday - February 23, 2010

Some time ago, I thoroughly enjoyed speaking to some fine coaches at the Wisconsin State Fastpitch Coaches Association. Discussing game strategy, I listed *four fabulous factors* that coaches must consider in making decisions: your team, the other team, the situation, and the conditions. Very recently, the second factor came to light on two occasions. I had read the complaints of a successful basketball coach whose team won by score of 17-14, but who thought it unsportsmanlike that the other team had held the ball for LONG periods of time. I also read of my favorite sports psychologist's (Ken Ravizza) work with the U.S. Army. One item in that story reminded us that "**the enemy has a vote**." Yes, one of the critical concepts that we have to accept in sports, business, and life is that there is normally the *other team factor* and they have the right to vote. Our job is always to better understand that factor, adjust effectively, and be successful in spite of it.

The enemy shall not outwit him; the wicked shall not humble him. Psalm 89:22 ESV

Tuesday - March 2, 2010

Let's talk about words. A *Wannabe PHD* once told me that he had a paper returned with a note advising him to "make it more academic." My experiences in education tell me that this means the advisor wanted him to make it less understandable. Like the second grader who could not understand a teacher's basic subtraction instruction to "cross out and *carry*" until his classmate said, "You dummy, just cross that out and then *tote* it over there," we often fail to understand the written or spoken message because someone uses the wrong words. In athletics and many other fields, we must frequently be reminded that our words normally have a goal of reinforcing or changing thoughts and actions. We must not only say it so that people understand it with their head…we must say it so they actually **understand it with their hands and feet**. Even if you have to *tote* this thought around with you to *carry* out the intent, so be it. Word choice is critical!

Then Jesus' disciples said, "Now you are speaking clearly and without figures of speech. Now we can see that you know all things and that you do not even need to have anyone ask you questions. This makes us believe that you came from God." John 16:29-30 NIV

Tuesday - March 9, 2010

A mother that I know well was justifiably feeling overwhelmed when Carly, her college age daughter, said, "You've got to de-stress." Mama answered, "What can I do? I'm just not sure where to start." Wise young Carly replied, "Just pick one thing and ATTACK it. Then go to the next one." At that specific moment, it was very simple, very solid advice that we all should place in our de-stress kit. At the same time, let's be careful not to clone our response to stress. It was the right one for that person in that situation, but there can be other choices. Multitasking or toggling, as discussed by Vince Poscente in *The Age Of Speed,* can work if we allow speed-increasing disruptions. We also may choose to do two things at a time, like running bases wearing a fielder's glove so we practice both offense and defense. Focus an attack on one item, multitask, toggle, or do more than one thing at a time…all work. The **de-stress choice** is yours.

Then He arose and rebuked the wind, and said to the sea, "Peace, be still!" And the wind ceased and there was a great calm. Mark 4:39 NKJV

Tuesday - March 16, 2010

NOW. Just three letters, but it's a very interesting word. It's a divider, separating the past from the future. In sports and life, we can discuss the times of before NOW, NOW, and after NOW. Most sports psychologists emphasize focusing on the NOW, but when my wife asks me to do something, she wants it done before NOW. I haven't figured out how to do that yet, but possibly in the after NOW time period, I'll get better at it. I once read in *Joe Torre's Ground Rules for Winners* that Hank Aaron, the great home run hitter, said, "Each at-bat is a new day." We should definitely learn from the past and confidently project the future, but we should not get stuck in either place. Instead, we should find joy in the fact that each at-bat in baseball or softball, as well as each moment in life, allows a fresh start. Start NOW improving your skill at dealing with the **NOW** moments. Along the way, if you learn how to do something before NOW, let me know.

For He says: "In an acceptable time I have heard you, And in the day of salvation I have helped you." Behold, now is the accepted time; behold, now is the day of salvation. 2 Corinthians 6:2 NKJV

Tuesday - March 23, 2010

A key item that I emphasize in hitting mechanics is an inside path of the hands (hands stay close to the body until extension late in the swing), as opposed to barring out, casting, or sweeping the bat in a longer path. I thought about that recently when I studied a Sunday School lesson, as well as when I heard a commercial telling me about a quick and easy way to learn a foreign language. In hitting, I prefer the quicker, seemingly more explosive inside path. In our culture, most people seem to be looking for the quicker, easier path to everything from gaining wealth, learning a language, achieving a position at their work, taking a GPS enabled trip, or getting a food order. Be careful! Sometimes, we need the struggle, challenge, and maturing that the longer trip may provide. In these cases, hitting the ball hard in softball may not be the same as hitting it well in life. Be wise, patient, and persevering as you choose **your paths** and make your journeys.

When Pharaoh finally let the people go, God did not lead them along the main road that runs through Philistine territory, even though that was the shortest route to the Promised Land…So God led them in a roundabout way through the wilderness toward the Red Sea… Exodus 13:17-18 NLT

Tuesday - March 30, 2010

On a 2001 flight to work with the Greek National Softball Team, I was seated beside a young professional opera singer on her way to perform in Greece. I hate opera, but realized that she was an elite performer and that she could likely share some thoughts to help me coach elite softball performers. That she did and I'll share just one lesson here. She said that, in addition to singing, she also taught voice lessons. With a glow on her face, I saw the passion for teaching in her heart as she explained how teaching had helped her so much to better understand what her teachers had taught her when she attended Juilliard. She said that earlier she had been able to perform, but the understanding brought about by teaching others had allowed her to perform so much better. Why we do not apply this principle more in our coaching in softball, education, business, or so many other places befuddles me. Teach them to *learn better by teaching others*.

And the things that you have heard from me among many witnesses, commit these to faithful men who will be able to teach others also.
2 Timothy 2:2 NKJV

Tuesday - April 6, 2010

It's getting warmer, so it has to be the time of year when tons of softball and baseball teams are wondering who will be the one that ends up Number 1. We know that it is extremely difficult to end up on top, whether we seek a World Series ring, valedictorian honor, or largest market share. As difficult as it may be to win the top prize, maintaining that level is likely even harder. Like mutual funds, **past performance is no guarantee of future success**. Battling recent success is often even tougher than overcoming defeat. Relief, relaxation, and too high a value on the pats-on-the-back can lead to complacency, arrogance, and decline for athletes, students, businesses, and nations. We must teach others and ourselves to remember how we got there. We must then determine to work harder and smarter to get even better, knowing that what got you to that point will rarely get you to the next points. Battle to get there. After you get there, battle even harder.

In the race to success, there is no finish line. It constantly outdistances us...You cannot let down in preparation, conditioning, or psychological readiness. Mike Shanahan

Tuesday - April 13, 2010

She was not the best player at the clinic, but she got my attention when she worked on her own during the break. She was practicing throwing, trying to internalize what she had just seen. Later, I saw her practice outfield footwork. Quickly, she was feeling the difference in her old way versus what she had just been taught. In a home run derby drill to get hitters to attack the ball, she got frustrated. She was just starting to play and had little chance to match the veteran players. Some saw a player of below average skill. I saw a young girl with an inspiring teachable spirit, fantastic attitude, and all-out effort. I knelt in front of her, put my hands on her shoulders, looked her right in the eyes, and told her that she was *the best practicer* (my word) in the whole clinic. Given a new goal, she went back to work, building a foundation for future success in life. Look around your field, business, or classroom and find these people, for they are the **true winners**.

Whatever you have learned or received or heard from me, or seen in me—put it into practice. And the God of peace will be with you. Philippians 4:9 NIV

Tuesday - April 20, 2010

In sports and many other fields, we seem to like words like *work*, *hustle*, *aggressive*, and *busy*. Unfortunately, without the proper adjective, these words can be very misleading and often even have a negative effect. Hard work, by itself, may produce little of value. Cutting down a large oak tree with a pocketknife is very hard work, but also dumb. We need to have a proper purpose and plan, and then work both **hard and smart**. A baserunner who makes the last out of a game at home and sees her team lose 10-0 is guilty of dumb hustle. The same runner being out trying to break the tie with two outs in the bottom of the seventh could possibly be using smart hustle. A hitter really attacking a pitch could be smart aggressive or dumb aggressive, based on factors such as the count, pitch location, score, and inning. Staying busy at work sounds good, but may not be if we're busy doing the wrong things. Check the adjectives where you play or work.

Doing more does not necessarily mean doing better.

Tuesday - April 27, 2010

In a recent blog, Jim Duggan, my pastor, quoted Dr. Tony Evans, a well-known pastor in Texas. The quote (see below) and blog stirred my thoughts again about the concept of **awareness**, a quality I often see lacking in athletes, students, and myself on many occasions. Too often, we just do not have quality awareness of what is going on around us. If you have doubts, go drive on a crowded highway and see how many people are seemingly oblivious to other drivers. To help in my world, I plan to start including "Situational Awareness" as a topic in our softball camps for elite players. We will work to improve use of the past, thorough examination of the present, and better expectation, visualization, and preparation for the future. We'll strive to escape the *prison of familiarity*, deal better with surprises, and adjust our actions based on increased awareness. Join us wherever you are and learn to faithfully and confidently "see the unseen." Thanks, Jim, for your blog.

If all you see is what you see then you will never see all there is to be seen.
Dr. Tony Evans

Tuesday - May 4, 2010

While coaching baseball in the 1970's at Florida State, I had thoughts of getting married someday and I would pray that God would provide someone who would be **good to me and good for me**. Boy, did He send a divinely wonderful answer to that prayer! Despite thousands and thousands of females on the FSU campus, He instead led me to my future wife Bonnie, who lived in Ty Ty, Georgia (2000 population of 716). As we consider our mothers and the mothers of our children, it's clear she has been fantastic. She has definitely been good to our daughter Neilie and me and likewise good for us. Often, the *good tos* seem more fun than the *good* *fors*, but the *good fors* are often more helpful than the *good tos*. She is nice enough to be good to us and courageous enough to be good for us. As a coach, player, teacher, student, employer, employee, parent, or child, challenge yourself to be both good to and good for everyone that you meet.

A wife of noble character who can find? She is worth far more than rubies. Her husband has full confidence in her and lacks nothing of value. Proverbs 31:10-11 NIV

Tuesday - May 11, 2010

In their book *Switch*, brothers Chip and Dan Heath strive to help us "change things when change is hard." They mention a psychologist who found 558 emotion words in the English language and discovered that 62 percent of them were negative. Another study of over 200 articles led the researchers to conclude that "bad is stronger than good." They even found that people are far more likely to use negative terms to interpret sporting events or the day they just had. In my experience with softball players, they definitely dwell much more on what they think they did wrong than on the good stuff they did. As a coach, employer, parent, or whatever you are, do you always search for what was done wrong or do you seek to repeat what was done well? Are you **problem focused or solution focused**? To create significant change in ourselves and in others, maybe we need to "switch from archeological problem solving to bright-spot evangelizing."

Finally, brethren, whatever things are true, whatever things are noble, whatever things are just, whatever things are pure, whatever things are lovely, whatever things are of good report, if there is any virtue and if there is anything praiseworthy—meditate on these things. Philippians 4:8 NKJV

Tuesday - May 18, 2010

Carie Dever-Boaz pitched in three College World Series championships, was SEC Coach of the Year, and NPF Coach of the Year. Macie is her toddler daughter and one of the first phrases she spoke was "Go away," which can actually be good advice if applied to negative distractions or actions. The problem comes when we suggest *blocking out* as the best method for making them go away. I recently even read a state document offering advice to students taking standard tests, "Try to *block out* whatever is going on around you." Efforts to *block out* may just intensify the distraction. Watch what coaches do when they want something to go away. They **substitute**...relief pitcher, pinch hitter, pinch runner, or substitute fielder. Good parents use a similar strategy...substituting a desired activity for one they don't want from their child. Consider replacing a negative thought or action with a positive substitute. Help the bad to **go away**.

The bricks have fallen down, But we will rebuild with hewn stones; The sycamores are cut down, But we will **replace** *them with cedars* (emphasis added). Isaiah 9:10 NKJV

Tuesday - May 25, 2010

I spend quite a bit of time helping athletes and others deal with **fear**. The inability to properly recognize and use fear can easily overcome a skill advantage and lead to defeat when victory should occur. I recently read a quote by leadership guru Steve Farber, who gave some very helpful advice for any of us that encounter this emotion. Farber said, "fear can save your life or keep you from doing something stupid, but avoiding it can also keep you from doing something great, from learning something new, and from growing as a human being." The elite hitter must learn to confront and use fear in a positive way. She must recognize that fear is present and know that it can provide an opportunity for *learning moments* and fantastic achievements. She must practice properly, so that she has the confidence to trust herself to grow through the fear, thus increasing the odds of doing something great. By the way, this applies to all of us, not just hitters.

What matters most is how well you walk through the fire. Charles Bukowski

Tuesday - June 1, 2010

Opportunities to learn are all around us. Recently, I was reminded of the importance of adjusting. The *teachable moment* came when our deacons were serving Communion at our small Baptist church. Four of us were supposed to walk down four aisles passing the trays along those pews. Instead of two on each side, one man went the wrong direction and three were on one side and I was alone on the other. We adjusted, walking unusual paths, and at the end everyone was served a symbolic wafer. When it was time to serve the juice, we adjusted better and used the expected manner. I also saw a teenage girl, sitting with her grandmother and little sister, adjust and hold the tray the entire time for them so there was less chance of an accident. Small items? Maybe. Maybe not. **Little adjustments** often allow us to get the core mission accomplished, whether it is hitting a softball, reaching someone with a message, making a sale, or solving a personal issue.

And he said: "Truly I tell you, unless you change and become like little children, you will never enter the kingdom of heaven." Matthew 18:3 NIV

Tuesday - June 8, 2010

One of the greatest MLB hitters of all time was Ted Williams, who in 1941 was the last person to hit over .400 in a season. In the summer of 1972, I worked for the Kansas City Royals Baseball Academy and Ted Williams spoke to their players and coaches a few months before I started there. I religiously watched and read all the instructional material at the academy and his items were easily some of the best. He said that he used to ask all the best hitters what he needed to do to be 'great. In the end, he decided that the most important thing was to *"Get A Good Ball To Hit."*

To him, more important than all the stuff about feet, knees, hips, elbows, and hands were the **recognition and decision** of which pitch to hit. Contained in his six words are lessons for all of us, including (1) ask the right people a lot of questions, (2) personalize the answers by blending their *guru thoughts* with your own experience, and (3) actually do what you discover. TW did.

Plans fail for lack of counsel, but with many advisers they succeed.
Proverbs 15:22 NIV

Tuesday - June 15, 2010

I get a little perturbed with suggestions to use certain steps to success, or absolutes, when the number reaches ten or more. I actually like the number of items to be five or less, but might stretch it one or two more if it's packaged so I can remember them…and they actually work. I guess that's why I'm getting ready to mention the book *Switch* (Chip and Dan Heath) again. They mention **humble checklists** as a method involved in shaping a path for change. They cite Dr. Peter Pronovost of John Hopkins and his simple five-part checklist for preventing IV line infections and how, in just 18 months, it saved about $175 million and nearly 1500 lives in the ICU's of one state. They also note that the pre-flight checklist for a 747 is less than one page long. Maybe when working with hitters, pitchers, classroom students, or on most any project, we would be more successful if we began by simplifying and *humbleizing* (my word) the checklists.

Be on your guard; stand firm in the faith; be courageous; be strong.
1 Corinthians 16:13 NIV

Tuesday - June 22, 2010

In 2001, sitting in DeBilt, Holland, Craig Montvidas, Head Coach of the inaugural Greek National Softball Team, and an assistant (me) discussed our last roster slot for the European Championships. He wanted Player A, I wanted Player B, and when we finished talking, he chose Player B. In

2003, sitting in Macerata, Italy, I was Head Coach of the British National Team and my very loyal assistant (Ian Van den Berg) and I both thought Pitcher A should start a key game in an Olympic Qualifier. Our pitching coach (Montvidas) wanted Pitcher B. I chose Pitcher B. In the 2010 NCAA World Series, Arizona coach Mike Candrea let pitching coach Teresa Wilson decide to pitch to UCLA's red-hot Megan Langenfeld. When my daughter's father-in-law passed away, the owner and a dozen others from J.T. Turner Construction, where she is Marketing Director, made the out-of-town trip to the services. Yes, true **loyalty** runs both directions.

I have a lot of confidence in what Coach (Teresa) Wilson does. That's the role she's in. I give her the opportunity to call the game. Mike Candrea

Tuesday - June 29, 2010

In *How To Be Like Coach Wooden*, Pat Williams explained how critical *keeping your word* was to the late UCLA basketball coach. During one NBC interview in his office, he ended the unfinished taping at exactly 2:55. The producer protested that they were not through and that practice did not start until 3:30. Wooden announced that he went to sit in the bleachers every day before practice at 3:00 so any player could visit with him and discuss whatever they liked. When the producer asked how many came for that, Wooden replied, "That doesn't matter. The important thing is that they know I'm there, in case they want to talk to me about anything." Widely recognized as one of the most outstanding coaches of all time in any sport, Coach Wooden exuded honesty and dependability. Would you or I have stopped an interview with a major network so we could **keep our word** to our players, employees, or family members?

Let integrity and uprightness preserve me, For I wait for You. Psalm 25:21 NKJV

Tuesday - July 6, 2010

In 1996, I bought *The Performance Edge* (Robert K. Cooper) at an outlet bookstore in Florida. My wife likes the cover, so it still sits on a bookshelf in our den. I like the content. He quotes Stephen Covey advising those who delegate to first "create a clear, mutual understanding of what needs to be accomplished, focusing on *what*, not *how*; *results*, not *methods*." Oh, how I wish I saw more of that in athletic coaching, today's schools, and the business world. If leaders would just let the performer perform (play, teach, work), maybe the results would improve. Somewhere along the way, too many have decided to clone out much of the athleticism, creative teaching, and business individualism. If they can hit well, who cares about their knuckles! If the rise ball explodes, who cares about the grip! Let's know the athlete, student, or worker especially well, **loosen up on methodology**, and enjoy the pleasure of seeing various ways get the desired results.

Stand fast therefore in the liberty by which Christ has made us free, and do not be entangled again with a yoke of bondage. Galatians 5:1 NKJV

Tuesday - July 13, 2010

I'm always been a little puzzled why softball players often yell, "Up, up, up," to let a catcher know that a ball has been popped in the air. I'm quite sure most catchers know the ball is up. What they need to know is the specific location of the UP (front, back, first base, third base, or whatever). Similarly, when a light bulb above us breaks or certain things are falling, some people yell "Heads up," when we really need to be heads down. And, when we are struggling or facing difficulties, our body language often exhibits a hung head. We need to look up and lift our eyes to confidently see the potential opportunity for *good* wrapped up in the situation we call *bad*. As a coach, parent, supervisor, or whatever you may be, watch what others are watching and see if their **directional vision** needs help. While you're at it, watch what direction you are looking. Maybe if we can improve the direction we look, we can improve the results we get.

fixing our eyes on Jesus, the pioneer and perfecter of faith. For the joy set before him he endured the cross, scorning its shame, and sat down at the right hand of the throne of God. Hebrews 12:2 NIV

Tuesday - July 20, 2010

In a 1994 newsletter, I wrote, "When coaching the bases, be careful about verbal instructions during the heat of battle. A runner coming around third base may not be able to tell the difference in 'whoa' and 'go.' The result could be disastrous. She also may not distinguish your voice from that of some fan yelling the opposite. Be visible and let her clearly see your instructions." If you watched many of the recent NCAA Women's Fastpitch playoff games, you saw several times where very good coaches were visible, but also very unclear and results *were* disastrous. As coaches, supervisors, teachers, and parents, we must educate others so that they clearly know what is expected. We must help them prepare for proper decisive action in the face of fear, tension, frustration, confusion, excitement, or other emotions that exist in their nitty-gritty performance arena. Finally, where possible, we must be **clearly visible** as we help them.

All this he made clear to me in writing from the hand of the Lord, *all the work to be done according to the plan.* 1 Chronicles 28:19 ESV

Tuesday - July 27, 2010

A few years ago, while visiting our daughter at college, we spent Saturday morning at a sorority softball game. Even with a number of quite skilled players, the game was primarily social and fun. As one player rounded second and headed for third, the young man coaching third, with a passion for winning, was clearly instructing the runner to slide. While running, she screamed, "I'm not sliding…I'm going to the beach tomorrow!" You see, what her legs looked like on Sunday was far more important than the outcome of any softball game on Saturday. Like that young female runner, we too must realize that current actions have quite an effect on future performance. In a world screaming for *instant gratification*, we must make decisions based on the fact that a pitch in the first inning can have quite an impact in the seventh inning. Know ahead of time **what's important in your tomorrows** and make today's decisions based on that.

To everything there is a season, A time for every purpose under heaven: Ecclesiastes 3:1 NKJV

Tuesday - August 3, 2010

At many camps, I conduct a session called "Using Focus To Conquer Distractions." Using lots of physical drills to develop a mental skill, we emphasize *substituting in* instead of *blocking out*. Last week, I personally practiced what I've preached. For many, many years, I have feared high bridges over water. As a boy, I hid from the fear by lying on the back floorboard. As an adult, I have chosen other routes or stopped and let my wife drive over the bridge. While these avoided the distraction of the potential for a collapsed bridge or my car going over the edge, they weren't exactly what I'd call **conquering the distraction**. Last week, to get my cute, cute, cute grandson to the beach, I gave in and decided to drive over a high bridge. I practiced as we approached, then bravely drove across it while focusing on talking to him, watching cars, and seeing the end of the bridge. Returning home, it was even easier. It works and now my wife says I'm a big boy.

And this I say for your own profit, not that I may put a leash on you, but for what is proper, and that you may serve the Lord without distraction. 1 Corinthians 7:35 NKJV

Tuesday - August 10, 2010

A neat word has entered my ears twice in the last month. At a summer camp, I asked a high school coach how she liked teaching in a certain school. She replied that, since moving there a few years ago, she had rediscovered the *joy of teaching*. Many teachers, struggling with tons of paperwork, meetings, and efforts of higher-ups to clone the people and process, are seeking that same joy again. Later, I saw a commercial about knee and hip replacements and the slogan was *Rediscovering Your Go*, meaning they could help you regain pain-free movement. Many hitters, struggling at the plate, need to rediscover an earlier confidence and once again attack the ball. Pitchers need to rediscover rhythm to once again gain velocity, movement, and location. Burned-out players need to rediscover the pure joy of the game. And, you may need to rediscover the joy of a job, a task, or a relationship. Best wishes as you seek to discover your own **rediscoveries**.

And when he has found it, he lays it on his shoulders, rejoicing. And when he comes home, he calls together his friends and neighbors, saying to them, "Rejoice with me, for I have found my sheep which was lost!" Luke 15:5-6 NKJV

Tuesday - August 17, 2010

Karen Marr, a wonderful friend and terrific instructor at many of our events, contacted me and told me that I needed to listen to a podcast with Olympian Jennie Finch. I am so glad I took her advice. Among the many jewels I heard was Jennie's reference to tennis great Billie Jean King's response to a question right before she played in her first U.S. Open. King said, **"Pressure is a privilege**." Sometimes, pressure can be imposed inappropriately, but far too often people try to overprotect others from necessary pressures. If I am ever on a plane that has problems, I want a pilot who can handle pressure. In a medical emergency, I want the EMT or doctor who is a master *pressure performer.* If my young grandson is ever in danger, I am glad that my daughter and son-in-law have had lots of prior experiences with pressure. Be careful not to overprotect a player, child, or employee. Thank God for pressure. It's a gift and a privilege.

For you have been given not only the privilege of trusting in Christ but also the privilege of suffering for him. Philippians 1:29 NLT

Tuesday - August 24, 2010

Have you wondered what Room 113 and Michelle have in common? The odds that you have are very low. Room 113 is an office in the building where I teach and Michelle was a catcher on the British Women's National Team that I coached. On the office door is a picture of three men fighting a house fire. The heading reads, "What's wrong with this pic?" During an intrasquad scrimmage in 2003, after only two at-bats against an assistant coach, Michelle, a former All - Big Ten performer, asked me, "What am I doing wrong?" **What's wrong** is our over-emphasis on what's wrong! Understand that I value correcting mistakes, but we spend far too much time on what is going wrong and not enough time building and using confidence in what is working right. On the field, in the classroom, at the church, in the office, and in the home, let's refuse to *over dwell* on what's wrong and instead discover, appreciate, and effectively use what's right.

Nevertheless, some good is found in you, for you destroyed the Asheroth out of the land, and have set your heart to seek God. 2 Chronicles 19:3 ESV

Tuesday - August 31, 2010

On Sunday morning, my wife and I took Cullen, our 18-month-old grandson, on a 40-minute ride in his little push car. We saw 5 kitty cats, a big dog, 5 birds on a wire, 2 jeeps, and lots of little water puddles. Just like he did on our Friday evening arrival, every time he saw these items, his little eyes sparkled, he pointed his finger, and his mouth often flew open as he exclaimed an excited, "OH!" The lesson…**oh how BIG the little things can be** as you go from place to place in life. Realize that softball defense is just moving a ball from place to place in a certain amount of time. Realize teachers need freedom to actually teach and move a student from a confused *huh?* to an excited *oh!* in a certain amount of time. If you can't apply this in your own world, then you need to stop and share a child's world for a while. Thanks, Cullen, for the reminder…and ask your mama and daddy to mail my heart back…it's in your front yard where you hugged me goodbye.

But Jesus called them to Him and said, "Let the little children come to Me, and do not forbid them; for of such is the kingdom of God." Luke 18:16 NKJV

Tuesday - September 7, 2010

My family seems to rarely get much time together at the beach, but, when we do, I always search for reading material. A month or so ago, I found *So Long Insecurity*, written by Beth Moore, in a condo at St. Simons Beach, Georgia. Only browsing, with a mental note to buy and read it all later, I found an especially solid nugget on page 12. Moore, a strong Christian speaker and writer, said, "I forget that in order to really want to go, something has to happen to make me want to leave where I am. Maybe we're all just sick to death of taking three steps forward and two steps back. Call me a math wizard, but isn't that still **one step forward**? Isn't that still some pretty big progress as we run against the hurricane of a godless society?" What about us? Are we willing to run against hurricanes on the athletic field, in the business world, or in relationships? Will we accept the three-minus-two math so we can move closer to where we really need to be?

The human spirit on its own is not strong enough long enough… Beth Moore

Tuesday - September 14, 2010

Last week, Richie Tucker, in charge of construction of a new building on the campus where I teach, told me that before they ever started building, they had to replace a bunch of bad dirt. He definitely understands that the finished product depends immensely on a solid foundation. Sadly, we neglect that far too often. A military officer once told me that plans must be built solely on facts and solidly supported assumptions. If an assumption is shown to be wrong, you have to start over. Physical hitting must be built on control of the body and all mental mechanics must be founded on trust and confidence. Regardless of the eloquence of the preacher, the true message must rest on solid scripture. Regardless of the credentials of the designers, any set of standard tests is an unbelievably poor foundation for a high school diploma or a teacher paycheck. Like Tucker, check your foundations, **replace bad dirt**, and build a better product.

Whoever comes to Me, and hears My sayings and does them, I will show you whom he is like: He is like a man building a house, who dug deep and laid the foundation on the rock. And when the flood arose, the stream beat vehemently against that house, and could not shake it, for it was founded on the rock. Luke 6:47-48 NKJV

Tuesday - September 21, 2010

When Dr. Fred Evers spoke at our revival, he discussed the difference in *having church* and just *going to church*. He said that having church involved (1) knowing it's happening, (2) talking about Jesus, and (3) reaching out and touching something bigger than yourself. Going is simply being physically present. I love the distinction. I feel that he was accurate in saying that too often we *go to* instead of *having*. What about softball practice? How often do players, or coaches, attend but not really experience what it's all about? Is the talk about softball or boys, movies, clothes, or music? Is it about the individual or about the team and how the individual can help the team? What about your job? Do you go to work or do you have work, actually accomplishing what the work is supposed to be about? Is there much concern for the company? Do you go to a meeting or have one that gets the right things done? **When you go, be sure you have!**

Jesus said to him, "You shall love the Lord *your God with all your heart, with all your soul, and with all your mind."* Matthew 22:37 NKJV

Tuesday - September 28, 2010

Little phrases interest me. Like, *iambic pentameter*. Tom told me it is a 5-beat rhythm and Shakespeare used it a bunch. Softball has rhythm, so this may be useful someday. A church book mentioned a *verbal hinge* and that made me recall what had occurred the day before. The *scriptural hinge* was *but now*. While I was handing out materials at a tournament, a local player came in and told her father that a blocked road had forced her to take another route in order to be on time. A second girl arrived and the worker told her she was late. She said that a train caught her, and then she leisurely walked to the team area. I wondered if the first girl had earlier told herself, "I have time, *but now* I better get going so if anything happens I'll still be on time." Did the other one think, "I'm late, *but now* I'll stop, tell my friend's father why I'm late, and walk on down to the team." Maybe she could run and be less late. Let's improve our **But Now** moments!

But now *you have been united with Christ Jesus. Once you were far away from God,* ***but now*** *you have been brought near to him through the blood of Christ* (emphasis added). Ephesians 2:13 NLT

Tuesday - October 5, 2010

I knew what I was going to write about today until I read the water bottle. Then I changed my mind. My wife often says that I read so much that one day my head will explode, so please don't dare tell her I'm now reading water bottles. The sticker bragged about using a smaller cap, which meant up to 20 percent less plastic and a reduced impact on the environment. The water was *clear*, but the message was to fashionably *be green*. This was okay until I read the warning, which said the small cap posed "a CHOKING HAZARD, especially to children." Do you think maybe the negative outweighs the positive? Like a groom in his wedding vows, I do! You know what? In softball and other fields, we are all guilty of efforts to change mechanics, methods, logistics, policies, or procedures where the negative outweighs the positive. Even if the change is fashionable and endorsed by the top gurus, watch out for the **very serious side effects**.

Jesus answered: "Watch out that no one deceives you." Matthew 24:4 NIV

Tuesday - October 12, 2010

Bookstores seem to be filled with items on losing weight. Well, Charles Stanley, in *Success God's Way*, was talking about a different kind of weight issue, when he asked, "have you ever tried to run a race with a fifty-pound pack strapped to your back…or run with your ankles strapped together?" I often see softball players who fail to achieve potential success due to such weights as fear, doubt, *excuse-itis*, procrastination, or frustration. Likewise, the same is likely true in people that you observe in your workplace, organization, or family. In another book, *Men Who Win*, Christian author and speaker Steven J. Lawson recalls that many ancient marathon competitors would remove their clothing before running. They endured criticism in order to get rid of any weight that slowed them down. I do not recommend their method, but we could all seek a higher commitment level and find appropriate methods for **removing mental weights**.

Therefore we also, since we are surrounded by so great a cloud of witnesses, let us lay aside every weight, and the sin which so easily ensnares us, and let us run with endurance the race that is set before us, looking unto Jesus, the author and finisher of our faith, who for the joy that was set before Him endured the cross, despising the shame, and has sat down at the right hand of the throne of God. Hebrews 12:1-2 NKJV

Tuesday - October 19, 2010

Wilbur, Jim, and I were discussing stents, those artificial tubes that doctors insert into vessels or other passages so that blood or fluids can flow better. The medical definition of a stent involves longer words, but I think you got the point. Wilbur's wife may need this procedure and Wilbur himself actually has six in his body. Jim's mother is way ahead with more than twenty. You know, we may need to do some personal checking and see if we need to insert some stents in the communication passages between us and other people that we seek to impact. Does our message to players, employees, family members, or others flow very well? Are the instructional arteries clogged and we don't even know it? Maybe, they are not just clogged outwardly, but also coming in. How well do we let messages flow *to us*? Is it time for a checkup, an instructional cath, if you will? We all likely need **communication stents**, maybe even more than Jim's mother.

The Sovereign Lord has given me a well-instructed tongue, to know the word that sustains the weary. He wakens me morning by morning, wakens my ear to listen like one being instructed. Isaiah 50:4 NIV

Tuesday - October 26, 2010

During this time of political races, I looked back to find what Bryan Flanagan wrote about ten years ago in a Zig Ziglar newsletter. He said, "You only need two votes to believe in yourself. Each morning, you must cast a vote for yourself. That is the big vote. Only you can mark your choice. The other vote has already been cast. God has already voted for you. He believes in you and wants you to do the same." A huge problem with most young softball players is a lack of confidence. At some of our camps, we even schedule a special session to deal with this. In addition, we seek other opportunities during all sessions to develop confidence-building skills. The main thing to realize here is that softball players, as well as people of all ages in other endeavors, get a choice. You get to cast **the deciding vote**. You even get to revote, with daily opportunities to cast your own ballot. Make it a habit to vote often and vote in the affirmative.

being confident of this very thing, that He who has begun a good work in you will complete it until the day of Jesus Christ; Philippians 1:6 NKJV

Tuesday - November 2, 2010

Robin Martin, an assistant coach at Nova Southeastern University, was a member of our International Player Advisory Board and attended many Higher Ground camps. She once told me that her team was winning in the semi-finals of the state tournament when a controversial call that would have ended the game went the other way. Robin's team ended up losing and she was very upset. When she got home, she went to visit possibly my favorite singer, Celine Dion, who was a family friend and living nearby in Jupiter, Florida at the time. Celine asked, "Did you guys give up when they scored that run?" Robin replied, "No, Celine." Celine Dion said, "That's all that matters, honey. You learned from it," and then gave Robin a big hug and a kiss on each cheek. When we get upset about the bad calls in softball or in life, do we give up or do we learn and improve? Do we get bitter or do we get better? Choose to **learn and help others learn**.

My brethren, count it all joy when you fall into various trials, knowing that the testing of your faith produces patience. James 1:2-3 NKJV

Tuesday - November 9, 2010

In softball, I often hear someone say that *so-and-so* has a lot of potential. They think someone will continue to improve their skills and become a top performer. Sometimes that happens and sometimes it doesn't. Some players develop into solid performers and some seem to have what we might call *permanent potential*, never getting close to the predicted level. There are far too many factors to discuss here, but three causes may be an unwillingness to stretch beyond the comfort zone, to risk failure, or to expand the assault on the obstacles and challenges that stand between potential and performance. Christian pastor and author Charles Stanley says, "I don't think anyone ever gets to the end of potential." I agree, but sadly some never even come close to the end of potential. He adds, "God has an **enlargement plan** for you. He wants you to expand on the inside so He can expand your influence on the outside." Begin your expansion plan today.

Enlarge the place of your tent, And let them stretch out the curtains of your dwellings... Isaiah 54:2 NKJV

Tuesday - November 16, 2010

Today, I brag. Our daughter, Neilie Dunn (Justin's wife, Cullen's mother) is the Director of Marketing for J.T. Turner Construction in Savannah, GA. About two years ago she heard that the ABC-TV program, *Extreme*

Makeover Home Edition, was looking at Savannah. EMHE finds very deserving families in challenging situations, tears down their sub-par house, rebuilds an amazing new home, all in about 106 hours, and provides other help to them and the town. **Very proactive**, she located EMHE's Director of Construction, telling him that JTT wanted to be the builder. For two years, she kept up her **passionate persistence** and **dedicated networking**. Two months ago, she was told that Savannah and JTT had been chosen. Last Saturday, I saw the 1600 sq. ft. house, only about 800 livable, go down. Thursday, the family gets a much larger, fantastic new home. Thousands of wonderful people are involved and YES, I am **one very proud father**.

But also for this very reason, giving all diligence, add to your faith virtue, to virtue knowledge, to knowledge self-control, to self-control perseverance, to perseverance godliness, to godliness brotherly kindness, and to brotherly kindness love. 2 Peter 1:5-7 NKJV

Tuesday - November 23, 2010

In a couple of days, America will again celebrate Thanksgiving Day. It seems that it started in Virginia in 1607, but became better known due to a 1621 three-day event with Pilgrims and Native Americans. It was officially recognized by President George Washington in 1789, when he appointed the day "to be observed by acknowledging with grateful hearts the many and signal favors of Almighty God." I am abundantly thankful for an unbelievably amazing family, faithful friends galore, good health, numerous memorable experiences, and people like you who read and/or share thoughts of mine and yours. Add fine young ladies who attend clinics and camps as they help me grow younger each year, and a game like softball that can be played in Bethel, Maine or Athens, Greece with the distances between bases, as well as number of outs, staying the same. Advice: stop right now, **be thankful**, repeat often. Did you? If not, reread and please do it now.

Enter his gates with thanksgiving and his courts with praise; give thanks to him and praise his name. Psalm 100:4 NIV

Tuesday - November 30, 2010

I do not know Laura Mrachek, but I did make note of the phrase she used almost ten months ago in a *CaringBridge* post to my niece and her family after my great nephew had an accident that resulted in lower body paralysis. She stated that she would pray for them as they adjusted to a *new normal*. I am still somewhat unsure exactly what is normal or how to adjust each time, but I am convinced that babies have to adjust to a change from normal crawling to the *new normal* of walking and running. Hitters may need to adjust to a *new normal* physical mechanic or mental approach, employees to a *new normal* schedule (may even be extreme for certain time period), and students to a *new normal* rigor in college. It may be fairly minor or very major, but we must choose to make the most effective adjustment to accept or overcome, whichever is best, and move forward successfully. Best wishes as you recognize and adjust to your ***new normals.***

Therefore, if anyone is in Christ, he is a new creation; old things have passed away; behold, all things have become new. 2 Corinthians 5:17 NKJV

Tuesday - December 7, 2010

I spend a lot of time emphasizing to softball players the importance of developing good habits. It may be about physical habits or it could be habits of thinking. No matter what, we are going to develop habits, so we might as well make them good ones. Habit development typically comes hand-in-hand with **repetition**. In a world that frequently seeks instant gratification, I see math students have trouble because they refuse to work enough problems to be able to recognize a concept and apply the right procedure to find a solution. The same is true with hitters who will not get enough true gamelike reps so that they can succeed when it counts. We run into the same issues in daily living because of poor habits of thinking. The thought process is flawed, so the action often fails. Pause and ask yourself where you need more reps. Then, repeat the thought process or physical action enough so you develop solid habits that work even in the tough times.

Repeat the sounding joy, Repeat the sounding joy, Repeat, repeat the sounding joy. From "Joy To The World," by Isaac Watts (1674-1748)

Tuesday - December 14, 2010

A softball clinic in Georgia one day, Florida the next, and a radio speaker the third day added up to the topic today. At the Florida clinic, I emphasized to teenage players that they should carefully observe their drill partner, play the role of a coach, and discuss what they saw. Too often, players just assist with drill logistics like equipment management, but never use wonderful opportunities to observe and share helpful information. We definitely need to improve the use of players as on-the-field assistants who effectively share with each other. Make that a big DITTO for students in classrooms and employees at work. One day before the Florida event, Terri Knecht and I did a recruiting seminar in Georgia and I began by saying that I wanted to share what I had observed all over the place through many years. On the third day, the radio speaker discussed the **joy of sharing**. Let's all help others and ourselves by better use of sharing. Do it well…enjoy the joy.

Let them do good, that they be rich in good works, ready to give, willing to share, storing up for themselves a good foundation for the time to come, that they may lay hold on eternal life. 1 Timothy 6: 18-19 NKJV

Tuesday - December 21, 2010

In his newsletter, E. Stanley Ott told of hearing Bob Oerter, a former pastor of the First Presbyterian Church of Boulder, Colorado, speak at a retreat. Oerter said, "Learn to live with the load of the **unfinished**." What a powerful piece of advice! Every time that I end a hitting lesson, conduct a camp session, or speak at a coaches' clinic, I know that I did not finish what I wanted to share. I accepted that fact a number of years ago and realized that my real job is to inform, inspire, lead in the right direction, and provide opportunities to *Get Better Every Day*. Still, I sometimes feel *the frustration of the unfinished* and need reminders from people like Bob Oerter. I imagine at CHRISTmas, some of you feel like you didn't finish shopping, cleaning, cooking, visiting, or calling. Accept the fact that you will not get all the stuff done. It's okay. Remember the true purpose of CHRISTmas.

For God so loved the world that He gave His only begotten Son, that whoever believes in Him should not perish but have everlasting life. John 3:16 NKJV

Tuesday - December 28, 2010

Algebra and New Year's resolutions seem to be a strange combination, but hold on. In Algebra, we look for a common solution to multiple equations in what is called a *system of equations*. One method for finding that solution is called *elimination*. Likewise, one of the goals of a resolution may be the *elimination* of something. I plan to eliminate the use of two words…*try* and *just*. An athlete, or anyone else, who says that she is going to *try* to do something, is often building in an up-front excuse for possible failure. It's normally better to say that you'll actually do it. The use of the word *just* can often limit the value of what it describes (heard a lady in the Kennedy family say this on TV). Examples are, "I'm *just* a recreation league coach," "I'm *just* a utility player," "I *just* pinch ran," "I'm *just* the receptionist," or "I'm *just* a stay-at-home mom." How valuable these roles are in their specific arena! Please join me in **elimination excellence**.

But now you must also rid yourselves of all such things as these: anger, rage, malice, slander, and filthy language from your lips. Colossians 3:8 NI

THOUGHTS FOR TUESDAY
GOLD MEDAL WISDOM FOR LIFE

2011

*But the **wisdom** that is from above is first pure, then peaceable, gentle, willing to yield, full of mercy and good fruits, without partiality and without hypocrisy (emphasis added). James 3:17 NKJV*

Tuesday - January 4, 2011

My daughter asked me to give her a book, *Parenting By THE BOOK*, by John Rosemond, for CHRISTmas. I searched the Internet, saw that it was based on Biblical principles, liked the sample pages I read, and bought us both a copy. Discussing change, he said "Times have always changed," and "Once upon a time, people understood that change would deteriorate into chaos unless change was organized around unchanging *still points*." He added that new technology being better than old technology does not mean that new ideas are necessarily better than old ideas. Rosemond stated, "there is, in truth, *nothing new under the sun*." While, he was primarily discussing parenting and the need to go back to much of what we'd call the *old ways*, a lot of this applies to where we are in athletics, coaching, education, ethics, business, industry, family, and much more of our lives. Could each of us at least look closer to find and use the **still points**?

What has been will be again, what has been done will be done again; there is nothing new under the sun. Ecclesiastes 1:9 NIV

Tuesday - January 11, 2011

Recently, winter weather forced a lot of cancellations at the Atlanta airport, where Delta has a huge hub. Hearing the media discussion of Delta flights made me recall joint efforts about twenty years ago. Along with Cindy Bristow, I was looking for the right phrase to name a volunteer coaching program for the Amateur Softball Association. I had decided that we could not truly certify much, so *certification* was not our word. I also knew that many adults would not want to be trained or educated any more than they already had, so *training* and *education* were out. Memory tells me that I was sitting in Atlanta, studying a triangular Delta logo, when I had the *co-thoughts* that almost everybody likes to get better (improve) and be a VIP. Putting it all together, we developed the **V**olunteer **I**mprovement **P**rogram, providing opportunities to get better and become a **V**ery **I**mportant **P**erson. Let's all strive to **improve each day** of this year.

Do not be conformed to this world, but be transformed by the renewal of your mind, that by testing you may discern what is the will of God, what is good and acceptable and perfect. Romans 12:2 ESV

Tuesday - January 18, 2011

This past weekend, we conducted our annual SUPER CLINIC with a fantastic staff and many fine players and coaches. Many of us ate Saturday's lunch at the Mercer University cafeteria and Beth Torina, the fine head coach at Florida International University, came to our table with an assortment of items. The most interesting was a plate almost entirely covered with small English peas. That especially caught my attention because I was planning to start a coaches session, "What Coaching Is Really All About," the next day with some tasty P's of my own. The coaches and I established a foundation for coaching based on **Purpose** (each drill, swing, pitch, meeting, etc. should have a solid purpose), a commitment to **Personalize** (refusal to clone skill mechanics, coaching concepts, and other parts of the game), and a flaming **Passion** (high-octane zeal for all parts of the game and the preparation). Beth and I love our peas and P's. I hope you do too.

But rise and stand on your feet; for I have appeared to you for this purpose, to make you a minister and a witness both of the things which you have seen and of the things which I will yet reveal to you. Acts 26:16 NKJV

Tuesday - January 25, 2011

One of my CHRISTmas gifts was the book *Action*, by Robert Ringer. I am a little over halfway into the book and it will not be an all-time favorite, but Ringer does have some really nice thoughts early in the writing. He highly values some components of success, saying, "ideas can be precious commodities…sound preparation is invaluable…knowledge and wisdom are essential." Then comes the *But*. He strongly states, "But ideas, preparation, knowledge, and wisdom are all but useless without action, because action is the *starting point* of all progress." I wonder how many fantastic ideas are buried in a cemetery because the idea holder never acted on them. How many players and coaches prepare well, but fail to actively apply the preparation during the game? Tons of knowledge and wisdom go to the grave as unwritten books and untouched lives. Pledge today to **actionize** your terrific ideas and make a difference.

Nothing happens until something moves. Albert Einstein

Tuesday - February 1, 2011

At recent clinics, I have frequently reminded hitters, plus coaches, that good hitting does not end when the pitch is hit, missed, or even not swung at. Whether it's a pitched ball or with use of a batting tee, there should be a "rest of the story." After the pitch or swing at a ball on a tee, the hitter should pause to **learn from what occurred**. Immediately before the learning phase, if necessary, she should control her emotions so she can properly evaluate what happened and how she can use it to be a better hitter. The "control of emotions" becomes vital when she gets angry, frustrated (awful swing, alleged bad call by umpire, or knocked over tee), confused, scared, or whatever other emotion might cloud clear thinking. Think how smart a hitter (employee, student, parent), we could become IF we briefly paused after each repetition to evaluate what happened and use it to perform hitting (or life) better. Simple advice, sure, but oh so neglected!

I applied my heart to what I observed and learned a lesson from what I saw: Proverbs 24:32 NIV

Tuesday - February 8, 2011

I've spent most recent weekends on the road doing clinics. I don't do ironing, so I carried a very small spray bottle of wrinkle remover with me. This past weekend, good friend Greg Riddoch, former manager of the San Diego Padres, and I did a private hitting clinic in Atlanta for four travel teams and a coaches clinic for a neighboring league. We had each team of twelve young ladies for three hours and Greg did a 30-minute video analysis of physical mechanics for two girls at a time while I had the other girls working on mental and visual skills. At the end of this wonderful weekend, organized by Danny Gershwin and Scott Farrow, I concluded that Greg and I were basically **wrinkle removers**. He helped them remove physical wrinkles in swings while I smoothed out mental and visual skills, along with a personalized approach to hitting practice and performance. Wherever you are, whatever you do, how well do YOU smooth the wrinkles?

as far as the east is from the west, so far does he remove our transgressions from us. Psalm 103:12 ESV

Tuesday - February 15, 2011

I read in *Be The Ball* (Charlie Jones & Kim Doren) that champion golfer Ben Hogan was speaking of "Karl Wallenda, perhaps the greatest high-wire walker in the world, who walked the wire between New York City skyscrapers…Wallenda was asked, 'Do you get more nervous the higher they put the wire?' and his answer was, 'Why should I? **The wire never changes**.'" I recall that Canadian pitcher Lori Sippel, prior to the 1996 Olympics, said that the crowds would be bigger, but she would know that it would still be the same distance from the mound to home plate and the number of balls, strikes, and outs would not change. The hitter must train to remember that the approaching softball is always the same size and no longer influenced by the pitcher, so the hitter is in control. The dollar amount may change, but the core of the presentation does not. The situation may change, but principles and truth will not. What a big trust builder we can get from a tiny wire!

Jesus Christ is the same yesterday, today, and forever. Hebrews 13:8 NKJV

Tuesday - February 22, 2011

Former President George W. Bush, writing in *Decision Points*, tells about an early experience during pilot training at Moody AFB, GA (about 45 miles from my home). Sensing Bush's insecurity, his instructor intentionally stalled the aircraft. After the plane shuttered, the instructor corrected the situation and it recovered. President Bush wrote, "He looked at me and said, 'Boy, if you want to be a pilot, you must **control** this machine and not let it control you.'" A former major league pitcher once told me that he grew up wanting to control a baseball, but at one point in his career he found that the ball was controlling him. As we start this spring season, let's be sure that we are controlling the game (ball, bat, schedule) and the game (ball, bat, schedule) is not controlling us. We can also ask the same about a job or other aspect of life…who or what is controlling? Lessons learned long ago in the friendly skies of Georgia are still valuable today.

For the grace of God has appeared that offers salvation to all people. It teaches us to say "No" to ungodliness and worldly passions, and to live self-controlled, upright and godly lives in this present age, while we wait for the blessed hope—the appearing of the glory of our great God and Savior, Jesus Christ, Titus 2:11-13 NIV

Tuesday - March 1, 2011

Are you contagious? So often, I hear someone ask this question to people who may have some form of the flu, a cold, another virus, or an exotic ailment like *oogooboogoo disease* (my term and likely non-existent). Whatever they have, we seem determined to avoid them and it. Well, today I want to inform you that they are contagious and so are you. As a coach or player, you have no choice as to whether **you are contagious**. Your choice is only whether to be *good contagious* or *bad contagious*. Being contagious simply means that you are capable of spreading what you have. You can choose to share bad items or you can share high quality energy, excellent work ethic, solid preparation (mental, visual, and physical), smart aggressiveness, courage, diligence (Jim's word), passion, trust, or strong commitment to a wisely chosen intent. Whatever you do in life, today choose to be *good contagious* and spread widely and deeply.

In this way the word of the Lord spread widely and grew in power. Acts 19:20 NIV

Tuesday - March 8, 2011

Tom Mark is the administrator at the school where I teach. He's working on his doctorate and, having only to tweak and defend his dissertation, he is *this close* (that is a very small amount) to finishing. Over the last couple of years, we have had some very interesting discussions about decisions that various leaders have made in education, government, athletics, families, and other areas. As you can expect, we do not always agree with those decisions or even with each other. However, the thing that I can *positively almost always* (that is very, very close to always) depend on is that Tom will insert the words *instead* and/or *suggest* into the conversation. He rarely stops with the flaws of the decision. If he disagrees with it, he likely says something like, "Instead, I'd suggest that he should have done *such and such.*" His emphasis is on **what to do** rather than on **what not to do**. I do the same when instructing softball players and coaches. How about you?

Come now, you who say, "Today or tomorrow we will go to such and such a city, spend a year there, buy and sell, and make a profit"; whereas you do not know what will happen tomorrow. For what is your life? It is even a vapor that appears for a little time and then vanishes away. Instead you ought to say, "If the Lord wills, we shall live and do this or that." James 4:13-15 NKJV

Tuesday - March 15, 2011

A few days ago, Cullen, my grandson who very recently turned two, was *gwocewe* shopping with his mother. He spotted a man in the produce section and very excitedly began to scream, "Granddaddy! Granddaddy!" Guess what? It was not me. Based on his side view of the man, Cullen had seen a head that was *hair challenged* and assumed it was me. My daughter loved sharing the story with my wife of Cullen's *false positive granddaddy identification*. You know, we often do the same thing in softball and life. The hitter sees a pitch, only partially collecting information, identifies it as a nice one just above the waist, swings, and then finds out too late that a rise ball has arrived much higher. Based on incomplete information, we hire someone that later turns out to be very high maintenance or even completely unsuited for the work we need performed. When shopping for *gwocewes*, pitches, or people, let's get **accurate information**.

So he began to speak boldly in the synagogue. When Aquila and Priscilla heard him, they took him aside and explained to him the way of God more accurately. Acts 18:26 NKJV

Tuesday - March 22, 2011

At a recent tournament, I was handing out flyers about our softball camps. The young lady at the gate and I noted that this was a terrific *people watching* area. So true in many ways! Early in one game, I noticed a small 16-and-under age infielder on a nearby field and admired her *presence*. She constantly focused on ground balls between innings and used them to work at her fielding and throwing, instead of *going through the motions*. During the game, she was always checking to see where everyone was (situational awareness). I admired what I saw and told myself that, despite her size, she might develop into a college prospect. However, as the game progressed, that changed. She became sloppy between innings, fielded balls nonchalantly, picked up bobbled balls with her glove, and threw humped-backed rainbows to first base. She exposed negatives instead of positives. Let's all pause to ask ourselves, **"What do others see when they see me?"**

In the same way, let your light shine before others, that they may see your good deeds and glorify your Father in heaven. Matthew 5:16 NIV

Tuesday - March 29, 2011

Today, March 29, is my daughter Neilie's birthday. I can't express with words how much I love her and how proud I am of her. Instead, I'd like for you to help me give her a very special gift, one that will probably cost no money (very rare for a gift for a daughter), but will be forever meaningful. Within fifteen minutes of reading this, I want you to **encourage someone**. It could be like Tom Draffin's (her co-worker) emails to me or Jerry Youngblood telling me that he's looking forward to me teaching Sunday School. Find the hitter that struck out to end the game, the pitcher that gave up the walk-off home run, the coach that may soon lose a job, a broken-hearted teenager, a receptionist in a big office wondering if she is important, a custodian who cleans up daily, or a person simply having a bad day. If each of you does this, thousands will be encouraged today. Call, text, email, or encourage them face-to-face. Your clock is ticking!

Therefore encourage one another and build each other up, just as in fact you are doing. 1 Thessalonians 5:11 NIV

Tuesday - April 5, 2011

You, Jim Duggan, Chick-fil-A, me, McDonald's, a board at school, and Jerry Lee Lewis have a common item. Jim is my pastor and he's likely to soon devour a Chick-fil-A banana pudding milkshake. When my McDonald's cup said to *Shake Up Your Day,* I made an effort to motivate online students with a board message stating that they could choose between a Mediocre Monday and a Magnificent Monday. Years ago, rock star Jerry Lee Lewis pounded a piano as he sang "Whole Lotta Shakin' Goin' On". Now, the connection to you! I'm quite certain that all of you can use **a little shake-up**. Can you liven up practice? Maybe hit some rotten fruit instead of softballs? Run bases with gloves on? At work, do meetings really have to be a cure for insomnia? Let's check attitudes, drills, formats, and routines. Let's get a *whole lotta shakin' goin' on*, ditch mediocrity, improve performance, and maybe even reward ourselves with a delicious milkshake.

for we have heard him say that this Jesus of Nazareth will destroy this place and change the customs which Moses delivered to us. Acts 6:14 NKJV

Tuesday - April 12, 2011

Sonya Thompson is the High Performance Manager for Cricket Australia. With dual citizenship, she was part of the British National Softball Team that I coached in 2001-2004. When I recently read that an elite female athlete said that her goal each day was to *Be Valuable,* I thought of Sonya. As a player, Sonya always made the travel squad for major events because she was valuable. Others could hit better, play better defense, and run faster, but Sonya could do multiple things pretty well, was predictable, rarely would do anything that hurt the team, and was willing to fill whatever role we needed (backup at several positions, lay down a good bunt, or run bases intelligently). Recently, still seeking to *Be Valuable*, she brought several cricket coaches to the USA in order to research *talent identification*, recruiting, and team concepts used by organizations like the Boston Red Sox and University of Texas football. What actions should you and I take to **Be Valuable**?

Look at the birds of the air; they do not sow or reap or store away in barns, and yet your heavenly Father feeds them. Are you not much more valuable than they? Matthew 6:26 NIV

Tuesday - April 19, 2011

When I taught at the local high school, a fine custodian named Ruthie always did a marvelous job and left our room much better than she found it. So that students would know and appreciate her, I always asked Ruthie's name as an extra credit question several times a semester. John Wooden, who won ten NCAA Basketball National Championships while coaching UCLA, said, "Many building custodians across the country will tell you that UCLA leaves the shower and dressing room the cleanest of any team. We pick up all the tape, never throw soap on the shower floor for someone to slip on, make sure all showers are turned off, and all towels are accounted for." I'd like for you to pause right now and ask yourself two questions. Is where you were yesterday **better today** because you were there yesterday? Is who you are today better because of what you did yesterday? Ruthie and John Wooden could always answer *yes*. What about you?

You visit the earth and water it, You greatly enrich it; The river of God is full of water; You provide their grain, For so You have prepared it. Psalm 65:9 NKJV

Tuesday - April 26, 2011

Recently, I made a technological plunge, buying an iPhone 4 to replace a low-tech flip phone that did phone calls and slow, slow texting. It was such a leap that a close college coach sent a *laugh-in-your-face* reply to my first message from the iPhone and a former teenage employee gave me that young look of wild amazement when he saw my new phone. Guess what happened when I started checking the calendar app? Nothing new…same days of the week as my old phone. It made me realize again that some stuff stays the same, regardless of the technology. Also, no day was named Someday, one of our favorite days for doing things in softball and life. But, the phone did lead to today's *Thought*, which became the catalyst for sharing the following thoughts (maybe original), "If **today** is important, then so is yesterday, because tomorrow, today will be yesterday," and "Learn from the past, live in the present, and lean toward the future."

Jesus Christ is the same yesterday, today, and forever. Hebrews 13:8 NKJV

Tuesday - May 3, 2011

I recently had two Levulan PDT treatments for *actinic keratoses* ("sun spots") on my scalp. Simplifying, they apply a chemical, let you hang out for 2-4 hours, stick you under a BLU-U light for 16 minutes 40 seconds, pretend your head is a chicken breast, and proceed to prepare fried chicken. It burns pretty bad for 2-5 minutes and eases up some as the treatment period winds down. The first time, the very nice nurse sprayed cold water and had a fan pointed at my scalp. The water helped…the fan not too much. The second time, due to longer wait time, the burning was more intense, but a veteran nurse added constant conversation to the water and fan. That *positive distraction* of conversation was extremely helpful. Coaches, players, others: here's the lesson. **Find what helps** the most and use it, realizing that it may be applied directly (water) or be a *positive distraction* (comments and questions). Know the person, find it, and use it.

that I may know him and the power of his resurrection, and may share his sufferings, becoming like him in his death, Philippians 3:10 ESV

Tuesday - May 10, 2011

How many times have you heard someone say something like, "Do one thing at a time…you can't do two things at once?" It may sound good, but it ain't true. Tanner Brown, an 18 year old who worked in our office the last two summers, provides proof. On May 13, he'll receive an associate degree from Middle Georgia College and on May 21 he will graduate from high school. For two years, he's been in a program receiving credit for both high school and college. He chose to **compress time** so that he could become an orthopedic surgeon sooner. Twin brother Taylor remained in high school and graduates with Tanner in eleven days. Different goals and different uses of time…both good. When coaching, playing, or performing wherever you are, look for the right times to compress time and the right times to single-focus time. Decide whether it's best to *Tannerize* or *Taylorize*. Both can work…it's the choices that matter.

Walk in wisdom toward outsiders, making the best use of the time. Colossians 4:5 ESV

Tuesday - May 17, 2011

I once asked one of our players on the British Women's National Team what she had done at work the week before. She replied that she had gone to a lot of meetings. To follow up, I then asked, "Well, what did you do at the meetings?" She said that they did what they always did at her company's meetings...they decided to meet again. A few years later, a very sharp colleague described such a meeting as that, or anything similar, as simply a ***BOGSAT***, which stands for **B**unch **O**f **G**uys **S**itting **A**round **T**ables. You likely have conducted or attended a do-nothing meeting, practice, or session of some type that falls into this unproductive classification. Check your practice session, your work environment, your classroom, and your personal work or workout space and see if it is purposefully productive. Determine to avoid bogging down in a personal or group *BOGSAT* and instead make a truly positive difference wherever you are.

But be ye doers of the word, and not hearers only, deceiving your own selves. James 1:22 KJV

Tuesday - May 24, 2011

This past weekend, I saw a TV ad that said, "Learn the game (basketball) from those who play it best." Sounds good, but ain't good. We want to **learn** the game from those who ***teach*** it best. Playing well and teaching well do not always go together. I have known quite a few good players who are also very good instructors, but I can name some very good softball or baseball players who do not teach the game very well. It is not a criticism, because their job was to play the game well and they excelled at that job. To assume that they will teach well is not a very good idea. Likewise, I cringe when I read that we should *benchmark*...see what the best in a field do and then copy it. Again, sounds good, but ain't good because we ain't them. A young lady does not necessarily need to copy Jessica Mendoza (terrific player, solid instructor, and fine lady) because she ain't Jessica Mendoza. Same goes for baseball, education, business, and most other areas.

For the time will come when people will not put up with sound doctrine. Instead, to suit their own desires, they will gather around them a great number of teachers to say what their itching ears want to hear. 2 Timothy 4:3 NIV

Tuesday - May 31, 2011

Georgia, my home state, recently enacted a tougher law regarding illegal immigration. It does not limit legal immigration, but was presented to reduce the cost of certain services to some who enter illegally. I read in the local paper that it was having a serious impact on vegetable farms located here. A farm leader said that owners were having trouble securing legal residents who would do the hard, sweaty work, even with unemployment near ten percent. A travel team coach tells me it is hard to find enough quality softball pitchers because it demands too much hard work to learn that skill. Some top NCAA softball coaches often state that many of today's college players are so involved in social networking and other activity that it prevents them from working as hard at softball as they should. Education, business, parenting, and more areas of life daily yield similar evidence. Maybe we should declare **hard work** an endangered species. Scary!

All hard work brings a profit, but mere talk leads only to poverty.
Proverbs 14:23 NIV

Tuesday - June 7, 2011

Bonnie and I took a mini-vacation with my daughter's family (husband and barely 2-year-old grandson) last week. Learned about **adjusting**. From Tifton to Amelia Island are all four-lane highways, but speed limits range from 35-70 mph. To avoid contributing to some local economies, it's best to recognize the changes and adjust. On Day 2, I saw barely 2-year-old Cullen also demonstrate adjusting. Scared of the BIG water (Atlantic Ocean) on Day 1, he now would sit with me and let waves crash against us. The day before, he had run from his fear. Now, he sat there, took some waves full force in his tiny chest, squealed and laughed at the BIG water right in his face, yelling "More" so he could again show that he would adjust and conquer his fear. So often in softball and life, we must face the fear, get back in the box or on the mound and battle toe to toe. Cullen, thanks again for a little boy reminder to an old man. It can help us all.

For God has not given us a spirit of fear, but of power and of love and of a sound mind. 2 Timothy 1:7 NKJV

Tuesday - June 14, 2011

It was probably about fifteen years ago when I last conducted a softball camp in Olathe, Kansas. While there, some of us decided to go watch a Kansas City Royals game. In my mid 20's, I had worked in the Royals system, so it was nice to get to see the major league team play. An incident that happened is still etched in my mind. Tim Salmon, an opposing hitter, looked really bad on a pitch, stepped out of the box, tapped his shoe with his bat, and got back in the box. I watch such *little things* and realized that it was the only time in the game that he tapped the dirt off his shoe that way. Sometime later, I was with Ken Ravizza, the sport psychologist for Salmon's team, and I had to ask him, "Does Tim Salmon knock the dirt off his shoes as his *release*?" Ken's answer was, "Yes." We teach players, coaches, and others to find some appropriate physical action to **release the negative** that just occurred, and then prepare again for battle. What do YOU use?

And whoever will not receive you nor hear your words, when you depart from that house or city, shake off the dust from your feet. Matthew 10:14 NKJV

Tuesday - June 21, 2011

This week, in our SELECT CAMP for elite softball players ages 14 and over, we have a combat veteran U.S. Army Ranger officer conducting a session entitled "Trusting Your Warrior Mentality." To me, the instructor, who was wounded in combat during an attack on his unit, is a hero who defends his country. The young ladies will learn that many principles used by elite soldiers also apply to elite softball players. The pitcher uses a $5.00 weapon to attack a hitter who has her $200-300 weapon. They battle over the air space immediately above home plate. The opponents prepare well for that battle, making decisions and taking actions in split - second time frames. That preparation and game action require a **warrior**

mentality and trust that must be practiced as much or more than physical actions. I encourage you, in softball and other areas of life, to look for principles that can successfully transfer to make you a daily champion.

The Lord will march out like a champion, like a warrior he will stir up his zeal; with a shout he will raise the battle cry and will triumph over his enemies. Isaiah 42:13 NIV

Tuesday - June 28, 2011

Last week, we exposed elite softball players at our SELECT CAMP to a session on "Asking Good Questions & Getting Answers," conducted by Greg Riddoch, former manager of the San Diego Padres. Two days later, I flew to the U.S. Virgin Islands to work with National Team prospects. Along the way, I purchased *Building Leaders The West Point Way*, by Major General Joseph P. Franklin, U.S. Army (Retired). He says that, at age 73, he still asks himself one simple question before going to sleep: "*What do I need to work on*." He adds, "So far, the answer has never been…*Nothing*. And I suspect it never will be." A few pages later, he wrote, "West Point produces leaders, and leaders must, at every turn, ask themselves the hardest of questions: *What are we doing…and why are we doing it*." As we build leaders on our coaching staff and team, or in schools, businesses, and homes, will we ask the right **questions** and get accurate **answers**?

Ask and it will be given to you; seek and you will find; knock and the door will be opened to you. Matthew 7:7 NIV

Tuesday - July 5, 2011

Looking on a bookshelf for something to share today, I picked up a little book, *Don't Worry, Make Money*, written in 1998 by Richard Carlson, whose claim to fame was *Don't Sweat The Small Stuff*. I'm not sure that I like either title, but the first one had a chapter heading, "Learn The Magic Of Nonattachment," that got my attention. Carlson said **nonattachment** "allows you to have fun in your efforts, to enjoy the process…helps you focus and stay on purpose…helps you stay out of your own way." Wow, do I see this all the time with young ladies playing softball. I think more hitters struggle with getting in their own way than they do with poor mechanics. They let the *boogie bears* (stress, fear, confusion, frustration, and other members of the *Emotion* family) in their head get in the way of the athlete in their body. Let's strive daily to let the athlete, and each other, experience *nonattached freedom*, enjoy the process, and stay on purpose.

Stand fast therefore in the liberty by which Christ has made us free, and do not be entangled again with a yoke of bondage. Galatians 5:1 NKJV

Tuesday - July 12, 2011

A few days ago, on a four-hour drive to a softball camp, I was listening to Christian radio and caught part of a sermon by evangelist David Jeremiah. He made a statement of high significance when he said, "the most urgent need of our day is **encouragement**." He was speaking of all the crises in the world and the struggles of so many people. I think that he could easily be right and his statement definitely also applies to many of the people that I instruct in softball. Many are discouraged by frustration with their performance, inability to please someone else, brow beatings and verbal abuse from coaches, parents, or teammates, and other similar issues. It is a critical issue in our game and coaches, parents, teammates, and others need to open their eyes and become more aware of an urgent need to encourage others. Start a contagious process right now on your team, in your school, at your business, and with your family. Be that ENCOURAGER!

Therefore encourage one another and build one another up, just as you are doing. 1 Thessalonians 5:11 ESV

Tuesday - July 19, 2011

Lilly Rossetti, a very fine lady and coach in Italy, alerted me to the website *www.mindtools.com*. One item on mentoring was entitled, "Build

Sustainable Improvements, Not Quick Fixes." Boy, do we need to apply that in our game of softball and very likely in whatever field that you are in. Coaches and players may look for short-term mechanical solutions, what we call *quick fixes*, rather than building solid, understandable, and adjustable foundations that will sustain the player through various levels of the game. We seek the *popular quick-fix, cloned fad* that is the hot item from the coach who is winning big at the current time, instead of learning solid principles that are sustainable. We may even do the same with personal relationships, and parents jerk kids off teams, putting them on weaker teams, so they play more, but improve less. Check what you are doing and see if you are seeking quick-fix answers or building **sustainable improvements**.

A simple answer to a problem is rarely as valuable as understanding how to approach such problems in the future. From www.mindtools.com

Tuesday - July 26, 2011

I often add a quote at the *end* of these thoughts, but today I'll *start* with one from Albert Einstein. He supposedly said, "Everybody is a genius. But, if you judge a fish by its ability to climb a tree, it will spend its whole life believing that it is stupid." We make that mistake a lot in sports, business, education, and families. We seek to make the great player into a great instructor. May work…may not. The same can be said for the excellent salesman or VP being moved into the CEO position. We attempt, often with disappointing results, to move a superb assistant coach along a path of coordinator, head coach, AD, principal, and superintendent. We take the amazing teacher out of the classroom and elevate him to subject area coach. Parents want the child cloned into a tree climber, when the child could be a terrific fish, but not so good at scaling trees. Let's be wiser in **positioning people**. Einstein had a pretty good point.

But the LORD *said to Samuel, "Do not look at his appearance or at his physical stature, because I have refused him. For the* LORD *does not see as man sees; for man looks at the outward appearance, but the LORD looks at the heart."* 1 Samuel 16:7 NKJV

Tuesday - August 2, 2011

Garry Kasparov (USSR) became the youngest-ever world chess champion in 1985 and held the title until 2000. In 2007, he wrote *How Life Imitates Chess*. I do not play chess, but I bought it last week for $1.00 and the back cover has some extremely valuable excerpts. One says, "Losing can persuade you to change what doesn't need to be changed, and winning can convince you that everything is fine even if you are on the brink of disaster." I will bet the farm (pretty easy since I do not own one) that you have seen one or both of those mistakes. We **change** what we are doing too soon because we are losing games and it doesn't seem to be working. We keep doing what we are doing while winning even though a very messy collapse is just around the corner because of our flawed philosophical foundation or overall strategy. Examine your team, business, school, church, family, and relationships. **Chess** may apply. I can't wait to read the book and learn more.

Psychological muscles atrophy from disuse just as physical ones do. Reminder from *How Life Imitates Chess*, by Garry Kasparov.

Tuesday - August 9, 2011

I am expecting an extraordinarily special person to arrive sometime Thursday morning. His name is Jack Ryves Dunn and he is the son of Justin and Neilie Dunn (my daughter). We will call him Ryves (pronounced Reeves), an older spelling of my mother's middle name of Rives...one Ryves likely helped translate the King James Version of the Bible. I KNOW that he will be unbelievably cute (like me) and weigh about 6-7 pounds (a little less than me). Even though he will cry some, he'll still be as fine a little boy as God has sent to Earth in the last 2000 or so years. His older brother, Cullen, is now 2½ and he has blessed us with innumerable moments of pure joy, so I fully expect Ryves to do the same. I've been working every day to improve my spoiling skills and I fully expect to be ready for the challenge. Why don't we **expect something extraordinarily special** when we enter each day, the batter's box, classroom, or work place!

Thank you God for the precious gifts that you provide me each day. May I be more expectant. Bobby Simpson

Tuesday - August 16, 2011

Reading a mother's journal last week on *CaringBridge*, I remembered my time many years ago at the Kansas City Royals Baseball Academy and, more recently, my days coaching international softball with Craig Montvidas. When a new class of players came to the Academy, our **only** hitting instruction the first week was, "See the ball well." Craig often said that the rest of the world stood still during a tournament as we focused **only** on that event. The mother, a friend of my daughter, has just started helping her 3-year-old daughter battle cancer. Her words were, "I worried ALL day about (*getting her to take*) the second dose of those meds…it was the **only** thing on my "to do" list for the rest of today…How crazy to think about 2 weeks ago I had a much longer "to do" list…errands, phone calls…cleaning house…goes on and on!" Oh, how we need to be able to shrink hitting, softball, and today down to **the only thing** that really matters!

Please pause a moment and pray for little Anna Hays Polk and her family as they bravely focus and fight their battle.

Tuesday - August 23, 2011

A teenage baseball hitting student and I have had many discussions lately about how he has grown up and adopted a more mature approach at the plate. Likewise, I am very proud of a math student that reappeared in my class with a much more grown up effort. Now, let's connect that to my 2 ½ year-old grandson Cullen's comment after riding in an elevator when shrill screams had made us avoid them for most of two days. He overcame his fear and, as the door opened, got out saying, "That not so bad!" Later,

I thought about little children who fight in the afternoon and then ask their parents to let them spend the night together. And, what about the little ones playing T Ball and their greater concern for post-game snacks in comparison to extreme parents who gripe about umpire calls, coaches strategy, and who scored the most. Considering fear, teamwork, game approach, and more, let's make ***growing down*** an integral part of growing up.

And he said: "Truly I tell you, unless you change and become like little children, you will never enter the kingdom of heaven." Matthew 18:3 NIV

Tuesday - August 30, 2011

Some time ago, I thought about a message on the topic below, but chose other items. This week, I saw a movie title that served as the catalyst to finally write about the concept of *enough.* Yes, I've heard more than **enough** stories of parents whining about coaches and pulling their kids instead of teaching them to battle for playing time. I've seen enough uncommitted players. I've seen enough coaches verbally abuse young ladies, often with profanity-laced language, for simply making a physical mistake. I've heard more than enough complaints about qualified umpires or tournament directors. I've heard enough students complain about material being too hard and parents blame teachers when their child's choices were most often the cause of failure. I've heard enough employees whine about work conditions. Yes, I've also heard enough of my own whining about many things that are a part of life. *Much is good, but we can all do better.*

Whatever you do, work at it with all your heart, as working for the Lord, not for human masters… Colossians 3:23 NIV

Tuesday - September 6, 2011

At times, my wife tells me that I go "On and on and on…" She is normally talking about the number of examples that I may give to illustrate a point. To personally reach each listener, I might offer too many examples. However, in softball training, as a coach or player, we do have to go on and on and on, doing it over and over, again and again until we can perform with excellence during all kinds of physical conditions and emotions. As Rick Eckstein, hitting coach for the Washington Nationals, told me about a major league season, "It's a grind." Successful players, parents, and employees are willing to grind it out. They realize that they will not achieve perfection. They know that the true goal is improvement and that improvement is often a moving target. The person that has perseverance or *stick-to-it-ivity* will simply keep going on…and **on and on and on**. Are you a better *stick-to-it-er* today than you were yesterday?

And not only that, but we also glory in tribulations, knowing that tribulation produces perseverance; and perseverance, character; and character, hope. Romans 5:3-4 NKJV

Tuesday - September 13, 2011

My wife and I spent most of a Saturday walking around Scott's Antique Market in Atlanta. Actually, I mostly followed, looking for books. Even with 366,000 square feet of space, we found nothing. Later, we stopped at a tiny, small town antique store and I found a 5"x7" book that the clerk said I could have free. It interested me for three reasons. It was entitled *When Do Teachers Teach*, was first written in 1934, and the author was Doak Campbell. I coached baseball at FSU…they play football at Doak Campbell Stadium. The former FSU President says, "Whether they will admit it or not, all people are to some extent teachers." He adds that teachers must always ask, "did they (students) come to know truth and make truth their own in a way to affect life and character?" Whether helping a softball hitter, toddler at home, student in class, or an employee, remember that **you are a teacher** and frequently ask yourself that question.

Teach them his decrees and instructions, and show them the way they are to live and how they are to behave. Exodus 18:20 NIV

Tuesday - September 20, 2011
It's no secret that we are surrounded by technology. I love some of it…I can instantly send this message to someone on the other side of the world and I can send it to thousands of people. Likewise, I instantly send or receive photos of two precious grandsons. Coaches and players can analyze high-speed action of a swing or a pitch and help someone prevent or fix mechanical flaws. I can search and find tons of high quality information about softball skills and strategy. But, we abuse technology with too much texting, too much searching, and too much dependence. Read what former world chess champion Garry Kasparov says. "A computer may look at millions of moves per second, but lacks **a deep sense of why** one move is better than another; this capacity for evaluation is where computers falter and humans excel." Let's wisely limit our use of technology, realizing God created humans with unique and awesome qualities.

It doesn't matter how far ahead you see if you don't understand what you are looking at. Garry Kasparov, in *How Life Imitates Chess*

Tuesday - September 27, 2011

Were you ever asked, "If Pete and Repete were sitting on a fence and Pete fell off, who would be left?" If you answered, "Repete," the question would be repeated. That saying reminded me of the importance of quality repetitions in learning to hit, pitch, field, and make proper decisions in softball, as well as in life. In turn, I started to think about some more *re words*, with the prefix that can mean *again and again*. So, today, let me **re**mind you about the critical need to **re**commit to excellence, **re**energize with passion, and **re**focus on the proper issue or action. To develop as a hitter, understand that an assortment of mechanics can work if you establish a **re**peatable swing and get your good pitch to hit. Along the way, from game to game, at-bat to at-bat, or even pitch to pitch, you may need to combine consistency with partially **re**inventing yourself. Then, **re**view. The *re words* above are multiple choice…pick one or more…use now…*Get Better Every Day*.

And Samuel heard all the words of the people, and he repeated them in the hearing of the Lord. 1Samuel 8:21 NKJV

Tuesday - October 4, 2011

Our pastor recently used the phrases *radical obedience* and *long-term commitment*. Let me cut and paste and discuss *radical commitment*. Tom Draffin has a radical commitment to managing a large prayer chain for J.T. Turner Construction in Savannah, Georgia and my grandson Cullen has a radical commitment to eating donuts from Mi-Lady Bakery in Tifton (I confess, so do I and my wife Bonnie). *Radical commitment* means passion, or really *getting after it*. I encourage hitters to really *get after it*. Many think hitting is a beauty pageant to see who has the prettiest swing, but it is actually a criminal assault on a ball. In their words, I want them to attack, smash, rip, bust, kill, murder, own, destroy, or crush the ball. Or, it may work better for them if they think of whipping, slinging, or driving the bat. I'm a non-cloner, so word choice should be personalized. Whatever, simply *get after it* in hitting and in life. Are you **radically committed**?

The LORD shall go forth like a mighty man; He shall stir up His zeal like a man of war. He shall cry out, yes, shout aloud; He shall prevail against His enemies. Isaiah 42:13 NKJV

Tuesday - October 11, 2011

A number of years ago, a major league baseball coach told me about a star on his team who had a quite obvious bad flaw (remember that I am about as strong an anti-cloner as you can find) in a major skill. The coach approached the guy and asked him if he'd like to know what he had observed. The answer was, "No." You see, the guy had terrific physical skill and was doing pretty well. A couple of years later, the physical skills had declined some and the struggling star came back to the coach and asked for help. There are several lessons here, and today I have chosen one that relates to wisdom from Ben Franklin, an American statesman, scientist, inventor, and writer back in the 1700's. Franklin said, "*Being ignorant is not so much a shame, as being unwilling to learn."* Shame on us when we think we know it all and are unwilling to learn. Today, let's be more **willing to learn** so that we can stomp out destructive personal ignorance.

Let the wise hear and increase in learning, and the one who understands obtain guidance, Proverbs 1:5 ESV

Tuesday - October 18, 2011

At the 2002 Canada Cup, Rosie Leutzinger got thrown out on the bases and asked me if she had made a good decision. I said, "Yes." At the 2004 Olympic Test Event in Greece, Jodie Cox asked me if I saw any flaws in her swing. I told her "You have a beautiful swing, so don't change a thing." Both of them were NCAA All-Americans playing for our British National Team. Rosie had absolutely amazing situational awareness and, even though I thought she had made a bad decision, we had just met and I definitely was not going to put brakes on her. Months later, I even told her that she should get thrown out *more*. I had also just met Jodie and even if I had seen something to change (I didn't), I wanted her to trust what she had at that time. There also have been times that I might have mentioned something to my daughter, but a stressful activity involving a newborn and/or toddler made me wait. Let's all remember that **timing is critical**.

To everything there is a season, a time for every purpose under heaven… A time to keep silence, and a time to speak; Ecclesiastes 1:1, 7 NKJV

Tuesday - October 25, 2011

A few days ago, after a terrific lunch at my sister-in-law Geraldine's, I picked up a little book, *Encouraging Words For Women*, by Darlene Sala. She wrote that someone else once wrote, "God put me on earth to accomplish a certain number of things and right now I am so far behind I'll never die." I've had that feeling and likely so have you. Coaches, we think we'll never get our team as prepared as it should be. To get more done in so little time, we study time management, talk to other coaches, get better organized, seek to compress time, *toggle*, and multitask, but still do not complete the millions of things we say we need to do. We find ways to get more swings, more pitches, more situational repetitions, and more game simulations, but are still not satisfied. Realize that **more is not necessarily better**. Let's all stop, figure out what our personal *its* are really all about, and do better at getting those *its* done with consistent excellence.

Yet indeed I also count all things loss for the excellence of the knowledge of Christ Jesus my Lord, for whom I have suffered the loss of all things, and count them as rubbish, that I may gain Christ. Philippians 3:8 NKJV

Tuesday - November 1, 2011

I started to write about topic #1, changed my mind to topic #2, and now writing on topic #3. This is football season and here the Georgia-Florida game is always big. Last week, Georgia won the game 24-20, but the local newspaper headline said it was a messy win and people tell me that Georgia, especially special teams, played poorly. One said that it wasn't pretty. I had two softball clinics this past weekend and I stressed to players that hitting is not a beauty pageant. The game itself does not give you any credit for a pretty swing, picture-perfect pitching mechanics, or terrific running technique. Messy or ugly is okay if you hit the ball well, get people out when you are pitching, or beat the throws to the bases. It really doesn't matter if the school is architecturally aesthetic. It matters whether appropriate learning occurs. Ideas with huge positive impact have come from messy offices. Let's be careful how much emphasis we place on **pretty.**

Your beauty should not come from outward adornment, such as elaborate hairstyles and the wearing of gold jewelry or fine clothes. Rather, it should be that of your inner self, the unfading beauty of a gentle and quiet spirit, which is of great worth in God's sight. 1 Peter 3:3-4 NIV

Tuesday - November 8, 2011

I used to hear it all the time as a young man, but rarely hear it now. The words were, "Set a good example." Seems like it's a good time for us to be reminded. If you are a player, set a good example by working hard and smart. Set a good example by refusing to let Facebook be a site for personal venting and team destruction. If you are a coach or teacher, set a good example by refusing to *cookie cut* instruction. Avoid favoritism and team politics. Students, set a good example by allowing reading, writing, and solid discussions to be your source of learning instead of YouTube, texting, and *he said–she said* hallway drama. Parents, it's nice to be both a friend and parent to your children, but set a good example and let the parenting aspect be a dominating priority. Employers, set a good example by treating each employee as a unique creation by God, not a spreadsheet number. May I **set a good example** and practice what I preach!

In everything set them an example by doing what is good. In your teaching show integrity, seriousness and soundness of speech that cannot be condemned, so that those who oppose you may be ashamed because they have nothing bad to say about us. Titus 2:7-8 NIV

Tuesday - November 15, 2011

About 6:00 Monday morning, I heard part of a radio broadcast of a sermon by the late Adrian Rogers. Its title was "Possessing Your Possessions." He said that you can have something, but not have it. That same day at school, a girl who asked to borrow a pencil said that she had a bunch of them at home. I said, "If you have a bunch of pencils at home, but you do not have one here, then you do not have a pencil." You must possess it to really have it. If a hitter has lower body strength, but shifts her weight too far forward or too early, then she does not possess lower body strength when she needs it, so, in reality, she does not have it. If an athlete knows when and how to be aggressive, but is restricted by fear at the moment she needs to be aggressive, then her cautious action indicates that she does not truly possess her possession (proper aggressiveness). I think we all can see where this happens in our personal arena and improve our **possession skills.**

God gives some people wealth, possessions and honor, so that they lack nothing their hearts desire, but God does not grant them the ability to enjoy them, and strangers enjoy them instead. This is meaningless, a grievous evil. Ecclesiastes 6:2 NIV

Tuesday - November 22, 2011

My daughter works for a major construction company that just celebrated 35 years of excellence in building and renovation. My 2¾ year-old grandson shows amazing focus and creativity in his engineering feats with various types of blocks. What fun it is to watch them as they joyfully develop their skills for *building up*! Personally, I am so very thankful for those who have helped to build up my life. And, I am thankful for every opportunity that I get to help build a hitter in softball, mentor a coach, help a student grow, and contribute to God's building project of my wonderful family. This is the time of year when we celebrate Thanksgiving Day and may we all pause to be especially grateful for those who help to build us up. May we also be thankful for the privilege we get of helping to build up other people on the softball field, in the home, at the work site, or in random settings. Determine today to be truly thankful and to get better at **building up.**

Let no corrupting talk come out of your mouths, but only such as is good for building up, as fits the occasion, that it may give grace to those who hear. Ephesians 4:29 ESV

Tuesday - November 29, 2011

Two days ago, our local paper, *The Tifton Gazette*, had a story about Judy Renahan celebrating her 100th birthday. On the same page, it highlighted Buck Rigdon's house, built around 1912, as part of the Christmas Tour of Homes. I love to **learn from the past**, so it was terrific to read where Mrs. Renahan said, "The bad times were our teachers." We need to be reminded that our current hitting slump may be a wonderful opportunity to learn. I read with interest that the Rigdon home had many more windows on the south side than the north, a method to help warm the house. As coaches and players, we too need to maximize facilities and space as we conduct our practices. So often, we overlook what came before us and we fail to improve like we should because we do not use what others learned in past times. Whether we are on the field, in the workplace, or at home, let us all allow our struggles to be great teachers and learn to maximize lessons from the past.

For whatever was written in the past was written for our instruction, so that we may have hope through endurance and through the encouragement from the Scriptures. Romans 15:4 HCSB

Tuesday - December 6, 2011

Normally, the first thing that hitters do at the plate is to determine pitch location. They ask, "Where is the ball?" Recently, our pastor stated, "It's a shame that *normal* is where it is." That's a very simple, yet profound statement. Maybe, we should locate our personal *normals*. Is it a shame that the normal work ethic on our field, in our work place, or in our classroom is where it is? Is it a shame that our intent or purpose is where it is? What about the normal level of passion for the practice drill, the assigned project, or home chore? Check your normal location and intensity of focus. Is it a shame that we allow our normal attention to be poorly aimed or constantly interrupted by distractions? Yes, we all need to check the location of our *normals*! Then, realize that the nice thing, unlike the pitches we face at the plate, is that we can convert our *now normals* to *new improved normals*. Become determined to **enhance your *normals*.**

Jesus answered and said to him, "Most assuredly, I say to you, unless one is born again, he cannot see the kingdom of God." John 3:3 NKJV

Tuesday - December 13, 2011

The last words in Lewis Colbert's book, *The Unlikeliest Auburn Tiger*, say, "There is greatness all around you. The world is a place of wide wonder if you just open your eyes and your heart to it...no matter what else you do, keep your head and your heart in the right direction and you will never have to worry about your feet." Dana Spurlin loaned me this book about a boy born with such a badly deformed lower leg that he was essentially without a foot. Despite that and other major obstacles, he became an All-American punter at Auburn and an NFL starter. His mention of not worrying about feet reminds us that two critical components of success in softball and life are content and direction. More important than our feet in a batter's box or on a mound are the content and direction of our head and heart. With mental toughness, creativity, and adjustments, we can overcome obstacles. Let's learn from Lewis Colbert and be sure to **keep our head and heart in the right direction**.

Jesus answered him, "The first of all the commandments is: 'Hear, O Israel, the L\ORD *our God, the* L\ORD *is one. And you shall love the* L\ORD *your God with all your heart, with all your soul, with all your mind, and with all your strength.' This is the first commandment."* Mark 12:29-30 NKJV

Tuesday - December 20, 2011

Fear Not! A few days ago, that phrase stuck in my mind and we need to explore it. To be successful at the plate, the hitter should *fear not* the strike out. To effectively work hitters, the pitcher should *fear not* the walks, even if her coach or parents scream about them. To be a really good baserunner, the player must use good judgment, but she also must *fear not* the out calls that will, not may, result from properly calculated risks. Likewise, the parent should *fear not* the yapping and/or temporary dislike that may come from a properly raised child. The business leader must also be willing to sometimes take risks and *fear not* possible failure. Far too often, we fail because we fear. To maximize our physical skills, to optimize our creativity, and to epitomize success, it takes **faith**

conquering fear. We may naturally be fearful, but we must replace the fear with faith, confidence, trust, and courage. All of us can do that!

And the angel said unto them, Fear not: for, behold, I bring you good tidings of great joy, which shall be to all people. Luke 2:10 KJV

Tuesday - December 27, 2011

In *Signs Of Life*, written by evangelist David Jeremiah, I read a discussion of early Internet days when many users were required to dial a phone number and wait for a modem to hopefully connect. Today, that is quite rare as most of us are always connected through more modern services. Jeremiah used this to open a discussion of being ***always on***. As we approach a new calendar year, coaches and players should strive to be *always on* instead of inconsistently *logging on* to the high levels of awareness, focus, trust, and energy needed to perform at our best. Neglecting to always be connected to the top levels of these qualities increases the odds of failure and will not *cut it* when our competition is strong. Likewise, in our roles in the church, the family, the workplace, or our relationships, we must strive for an *always on* approach. It's a choice that is ours and my desire is that we will all improve immensely in this coming year.

Therefore, my dear brothers and sisters, stand firm. Let nothing move you. Always give yourselves fully to the work of the Lord, because you know that your labor in the Lord is not in vain. 1 Corinthians 15:58 NIV

THOUGHTS FOR TUESDAY
GOLD MEDAL WISDOM FOR LIFE

2012

*A **wise** man will hear and increase learning, And a man of understanding will attain **wise** counsel (emphasis added). Proverbs1:5 NKJV*

Tuesday - January 3, 2012

My friend Paul DaCosta's latest newsletter has some statements that pertain to real estate investment, but fit us quite well in softball. He says that the year is going "to see the income gap between the have's and have not's grow…Hard work will be the deciding factor…pay attention to your surroundings, see what's going on and adjust…be prepared to work and adjust." Often, the gap between have's and have not's on the softball field comes down to awareness, hard work, and making proper adjustments. Actually, having consistent awareness is hard work, as is the habit of properly adjusting. Some have the discipline to be aware at times, but champions are intelligently aware a higher percentage of the time. Some adjust at times, while the best are intelligently adjusting more often. To invest as a quality player, be prepared to **be aware, work hard, and adjust**.

But Jesus, being aware of it, said to them, "Why do you reason because you have no bread? Do you not yet perceive nor understand? Is your heart still hardened? Having eyes, do you not see? And having ears, do you not hear? And do you not remember?" Mark 8:17-18 NKJV

Tuesday - January 10, 2012

One of the first baseball books that I bought was *Modern Baseball Strategy* (1955), by Paul Richards, manager of the Baltimore Orioles. He said to never bring in a substitute (relief) pitcher unless he could do better at that time than the pitcher you replaced. I recalled that recently and thought about other things we should never substitute. For example, in softball, *Never Substitute* pretty mechanics for results, an expensive bat for actually learning to hit, constant exposure for development of skills that coaches are looking for, or *teaching hitting* for *coaching hitters*. Likewise, let's *Never Substitute* profit for service, a good grade for learning, friendship for parenting, a diploma for being prepared, electronic communication for heart-to-heart talks, or moments of happiness for lives of joy. Let's examine our lives and begin now to improve our **substitution skills**.

So then, brothers and sisters, stand firm and hold fast to the teachings we passed on to you, whether by word of mouth or by letter. 2 Thessalonians 2:15 NIV

Tuesday - January 17, 2012

Our pastor recently wrote about Matt Emmons, who was only one shot away from a gold medal in a rifle event at the 2004 Olympics. He fired a terrific shot. The only problem was that he shot the wrong target, received a zero, and placed 8th. Emmons said, "When I shot the shot, everything felt fine." Softball hitters who focus too much on pretty swings and not enough on visual and mental skills often have swings that feel fine, but do not hit the target ball very well. Nice swing, but wrong location. He continued, "On that shot, I was just worrying about calming myself down and just breaking a good shot, and so I didn't even look at the number." He usually used the target number as a point of reference before lowering his gun to zero in on the target. To **score well** in all areas of our life, we need to select proper targets, follow a solid routine, and use effective reference points.

Since, then, you have been raised with Christ, set your hearts on ***things above***, *where Christ is, seated at the right hand of God. Set your minds on* ***things above***, *not on earthly things* (emphasis added). Colossians 3:1-2 NIV

Tuesday - January 24, 2012

Someone once told me that their high school football team lost a lot of games because they were unprepared. It reminded me that the motto for Boy Scouts of America is *Be Prepared*. Supposedly, the founder was once asked, "Be prepared for what?" and his reply was, "Why, for any old thing." I also thought of *exposure*, today's buzzword in travel softball. Players often overemphasize exposure and underemphasize preparation. The three components of success are instruction, game experience, and exposure. Unless one prepares well, the exposure is wasted. Relevant to being recruited, it is basically a negative use of time to expose weak skills.

Learn skills, learn to apply them in games, and then get exposure. *Be Prepared*. Finally, I thought of people who say that players need a will to win. Actually, more important is *the will to prepare to win*. **Be Prepared**!

But in your hearts revere Christ as Lord. Always be prepared to give an answer to everyone who asks you to give the reason for the hope that you have. But do this with gentleness and respect, 1 Peter 3:15 NIV

Tuesday - January 31, 2012

Focus On The Family recently ran a 30-second ad during an NFL playoff game between the Denver Broncos and New England Patriots. The mostly 2000 year-old script featured young children reciting John 3:16. At the end, a curly headed little girl exclaimed, "WOW!" It was touching as the children reminded me of the power of this verse and I loved the ad's concluding *WOW moment*. As I considered the creative ending, I wondered just how often we produce *WOW moments* when we coach or play. Do we enthusiastically stretch our skills so that we produce *flaming heart passion* and a Mary Lou Retton Gold Medal moment (1984 Olympic gymnast) or do we hold back a little and cautiously do *pretty good*? As a parent, an employee, or a student, are we satisfied with just *getting by*? Determine today to inspire yourself and others with **WOW Moments**!

For God so loved the world, that he gave his only begotten Son, that whosoever believeth in him should not perish, but have everlasting life. John 3:16 KJV

Tuesday - February 7, 2012

During a fielding session last weekend in Daytona Beach, Florida, I asked the young ladies, "What do you do first when fielding a ground ball?" I always get a lot of answers, but the one I am looking for is, "You move." I then instruct them to get ready to move before being ready to catch. Well, 12-year-old Sarah surprised me with the best answer I've ever gotten, "You find the ball." Even before you move, you need to find the ball.

Lately, I have not emphasized that properly. In life, we make the same mistake of moving before finding the ball. It's done so often in education, business, churches, and elsewhere. People develop a program or act without knowing where the ball is. We need to put the philosophical before the physical, develop values before taking actions, and establish principles before methods. Thanks, Sarah, for reminding us to first **find the ball.**

*But seek **first** the kingdom of God and His righteousness, and all these things shall be added to you* (emphasis added). Matthew 6:33 NKJV

Tuesday - February 14, 2012

I have read that Abraham Lincoln once said, "You cannot help men permanently by doing for them what they can and should do for themselves." I like that because it teaches personal responsibility. It reminds me to be sure that players carry their own bat bag, instead of letting a parent carry it. It reminds me to have players pick up balls and other equipment after practice since they are the ones who use them. It reminds me that an SEC Softball Coach of the Year once told me that the one thing she would change, if she could, would be making players have more personal responsibility. In softball and many other facets of life, we need to teach people to be more responsible. Oh, from now on, tell people that Rev. William John Henry Boetcker, a Presbyterian minister, actually said and wrote that, not Abraham Lincoln. **Talk about responsibility to get things right!**

"If anyone sins and does what is forbidden in any of the LORD's commands, even though they do not know it, they are guilty and will be held responsible." Leviticus 5:17 NIV

Tuesday - February 21, 2012

Cleaning up my office, I found some notes I'd copied from *Making The "Terrible" Twos Terrific*, written by parenting psychologist John Rosemond. He said, "…of all the features and psychological dimensions of the parent-child relationship that form during the first eighteen months of life, trust is the only one that will endure, that needs to endure. Trust provides the stability, the ballast the relationship will need to navigate the stormy seas that lie ahead." With all the emphasis on physical mechanics for pitchers and hitters, perhaps trust when stepping into the circle or into the batter's box is really the thing that needs to endure. The same may could be said for coach-player, teacher-student, employer-employee, and husband-wife relationships. Let's all spend more time in **trust development** so that we can successfully "navigate the stormy seas that lie ahead."

Trust in the LORD with all thine heart; and lean not unto thine own understanding. In all thy ways acknowledge him, and he shall direct thy paths. Proverbs 3:5-6 KJV

Tuesday - February 28, 2012

In the past, I used extra-credit questions at the end of math exams. One of them was a True-False item worded something like, "Based on the Simpsonic Algebraic Analytical Theory of Diffusion, a student who sleeps with his dominant ear on his book will absorb more information." Normally, about 20-30 percent missed it. You know, that reminds me of what might be called *personal diffusion*. I tell players to always pick the right partner in practice drills. Get somebody who will observe, coach, encourage, and challenge you. On the bench, sit with people who focus on the game and have a positive impact on your knowledge and performance. Yes, in softball and in life, it is very important who you hang around with (weak grammar, but strong message). Surround yourself with strong people. Absorb from those people who will help you *Get Better Every Day*!

As iron sharpens iron, so one person sharpens another. Proverbs 27:17 NIV

Tuesday - March 6, 2012

I once heard a teacher refer to the fact that many students today are *numerically illiterate.* Sad, but true. They know some numbers, but fail to understand or use them well. Also sad but true is the fact that many softball players may be *softball illiterate.* They may have great baserunning mechanics, but do they know when to attempt to stretch a single to a double. They may have tremendous quickness, great hands, superb arm, and courage, but do they know when diving for a ground ball is *dumb hustle.* Do they know when it's okay to give up a single or give up a run? Does the pretty swing get used on the right pitches? They may know where to find all the showcases and exposure tournaments, but do they know what to expose, when to expose, and who really has an impact regarding exposure. Let's all work to stomp out **illiteracy** in softball and other areas of our life.

And you shall know the truth, and the truth shall make you free. John 8:32 NKJV

Tuesday - March 13, 2012

I recently attended church in Savannah, Georgia with my daughter's family. Rev. Creede Hinshaw's Children's Sermon related to the 100th Anniversary of the Girl Scouts, founded in Savannah on March 12, 1912 by Juliette Gordon Low. She told those first 18 girls that they could make a difference in the world around them. Creede challenged the little boys and girls to also make a difference. How about us? Do we make a difference? You know, maybe a better question that we need to ask is, "What kind of difference do I make?" When I work with a hitter, is the difference I make good or bad? When we coach, are the differences made in softball skills and life skills good or bad? Do you have a positive or negative impact in your work site, classroom, or home? **You will make a difference**. That's not a choice. The choice you make is whether it's good or bad!

In the same way, let your light shine before others, so that they may see your good works and give glory to your Father who is in heaven. Matthew 5:16 ESV

Tuesday - March 20, 2012

I read where one state Department of Education's study showed a strong relationship between school attendance and grades. I call that a *DUH Study*, kinda like math rules that tell me that 4=4 or that when a=b and b=c, then a=c. Maybe I should conduct a study or write a book that shows a relationship between work ethic and success. If so, I'd recall that baseball great Ted Williams used to walk around San Diego as a boy squeezing a rubber ball to strengthen his hands and arms. Basketball star Pete Maravich dribbled a ball everywhere, even while sitting in aisle seats at the movies. Local valedictorian Kelly Murray used to study on the school bus at night using light from her cell phone. Look around your office, field, or classroom. Are the better performers possibly outworking, physically and/or mentally, others? Yeah, I think **work ethic** might be pretty important!

In everything that he undertook in the service of God's temple and in obedience to the law and the commands, he sought his God and worked wholeheartedly. And so he prospered. 2 Chronicles 31:21 NIV

Tuesday - March 27, 2012

I once heard someone in public education state that it seemed far too many people were *striving for mediocrity*. Despite increased funding, various programs, and standardized testing, this often may be the situation. Compare that phrase to one I first heard from Brent Strom, pitching coordinator for the St. Louis Cardinals. Speaking in December at a baseball pitching clinic we sponsored, Brent used the phrase *rage to master* as an ingredient of champions. On the Internet, I saw that psychologist Ellen Winner had written *Gifted Children: Myths and Realities* and listed this as one of three telltale qualities of gifted children. She stated that it allows them to achieve "flow states" and work through extended grueling training so that they could excel. I am convinced that we must explore ways to personalize this quality and allow more players to improve their skills.

Be devoted to one another in love. Honor one another above yourselves. Never be lacking in zeal, but keep your spiritual fervor, serving the Lord. Be joyful in hope, patient in affliction, faithful in prayer. Romans 12:10-12 NIV

Tuesday - April 3, 2012

Compliments (positive feedback) are best when sincere, soon, specific, and personal. Some examples are: Instead of "Nice game," use "I loved your preparation and awareness today." Instead of "Good hit," how about "I really loved the way you attacked the ball," or "You did a terrific job being patient and getting your good pitch to hit," or even "You kept your head down well and really allowed the body to be violent." Maybe "I admired your positioning on that hitter" is better than "Nice play." Instead of "I like your dress," substitute "You look really nice in that dress," and instead of "You look really nice today," say "I love the way you've done your hair." Tell the employee that "You energize the whole crew…it's just not the same when you're not here." That's much better than "You're doing a good job." We can all *Get Better Every Day* at **compliments.**

Gracious words are a honeycomb, sweet to the soul and healing to the bones. Proverbs 16:24 NIV

ABOUT THE AUTHOR

Bobby Simpson founded Getting Better Every Day, Inc. in 1989, basing the business name and purposes on the Biblical principles stated in the hymn "Higher Ground." A popular writer, speaker, and DVD instructor/producer, Simpson has personally provided services in twelve nations. He worked as an assistant baseball coach at Florida State University as well as a professional baseball scout and coach. Simpson directed the youth program for a national softball organization and coached international softball teams, including the British Women's National Team who won the Gold Medal at the 2004 Olympic Test Event in Greece. In addition, he served as a representative to the U.S. Olympic Committee House of Delegates. He was also a member of a blue ribbon panel that developed national standards for youth sports. Simpson spent fifteen years as a public educator and nearly twenty years as a leader in community and state recreation. A Baptist deacon and Sunday School teacher, living in Tifton, GA, he and his wife, Bonnie, have been happily married for 48 years. His daughter, Neilie, is the founder of Neilie S. Dunn Public Relations, living in Savannah, GA with her husband, Justin, and two *fantabulous* grandsons, Cullen and Ryves.

PLEASE LET ME HEAR FROM YOU

I hope that you found this book informative, inspiring, and very usable. Please take a moment and SHARE your thoughts with me and in book reviews and other locations. You can subscribe FREE online and receive our current *Thoughts* and additional materials. I look forward to hearing from you as we all press forward, Getting Better Every Day.

Bobby Simpson
Higher Ground
POB 741
Tifton, GA 31793
Website: www.bobbysimpsonbooks.com
Email: bsimpson@friendlycity.net
John 3:16   Proverbs 3:5-6   Philippians 4:13 & 19

HIGHER GROUND

I'm pressing on the upward way,

New heights I'm gaining every day;

Still praying as I onward bound,

"Lord, plant my feet on higher ground."

Lord, lift me up and let me stand,

By faith, on heaven's tableland,

A higher plane than I have found;

Lord, plant my feet on higher ground.

Written By Johnson Oatman, Jr. - 1898

www.ingramcontent.com/pod-product-compliance
Lightning Source LLC
Chambersburg PA
CBHW070150100426
42743CB00013B/2865